I0767124

CONFLAGRATION

Other books by the same author:

- **Betrayal** – A political documentary of our times
- **The Sands of Time** – Book of Poems Vol. 1
- **The Chalice** – Book of Poems Vol. 2
- **Nostalgia** – Book of Poems Vol. 3
- **Growing Up** – Children's Book
- **Conflagration** – A book of Topical issues in the 21st Century
- **A Book of Plays**

CONFLAGRATION

DOCUMENTARY OF A WORLD IN TURMOIL

SOPHIA Z. KOVACHEVICH

Copyright © 2019 by Sophia Z. Kovachevich.

Library of Congress Control Number:		2019912001
ISBN:	Hardcover	978-1-7960-0563-9
	Softcover	978-1-7960-0562-2
	eBook	978-1-7960-0561-5

All rights reserved. No part of this book may be reproduced or transmitted in any form or by any means, electronic or mechanical, including photocopying, recording, or by any information storage and retrieval system, without permission in writing from the copyright owner.

Any people depicted in stock imagery provided by Getty Images are models, and such images are being used for illustrative purposes only.
Certain stock imagery © Getty Images.

Print information available on the last page.

Rev. date: 08/26/2019

To order additional copies of this book, contact:
Xlibris
1-800-455-039
www.Xlibris.com.au
Orders@Xlibris.com.au
800431

Contents

Ye shall know the truth and the truth will set you free

John 8:30

For my family with all by love, thanks and gratitude

Anthem for Doomed Youth

By <u>Wilfred Owen</u>

What passing bells for these who die as cattle?
Only the monstrous anger of the guns.
Only the stuttering rifles' rapid rattle
Can patter out their hasty orisons.
No mockeries now for them; no prayers nor bells;
Nor any voice of mourning save the choirs,—
The shrill, demented choirs of wailing shells;
And bugles calling for them from sad shires.

What candles may be held to speed them all?
Not in the hands of boys, but in their eyes
Shall shine the holy glimmers of goodbyes.
The pallor of girls' brows shall be their pall;
Their flowers the tenderness of patient minds,
And each slow dusk a drawing-down of blinds.

The world is in serious turmoil and disarray. Peace, at the moment, is a pipedream. The causes we espouse are not worth losing our children, men and women for. If only we could accept that.

Preface

Every corner of the world is in disarray, whether it is political, economic, environmental or social. It is violent. This phenomenon is present in all our continents. It is widespread. However we look at the problems, they are very much in evidence and troubling. And a lot of the evidence is often concealed and glossed over. Still what is apparent is more than enough to worry us, to frighten us. The reason, in my opinion why we have come to this stage, is the deliberate sabotage and unwanted interference by the so-called democratic countries in the affairs of others. During the nineteenth century and before it was the Western *monarchies* that raped and destroyed mainly Asia and Africa and to some extent Europe. But that is old history. Now it is the Western *democracies* that bomb, pillage and destroy Asia and Africa and to some extent Europe! We shall look a little closer to our times, in the twentieth and twenty first centuries. In the twentieth century we had the US becoming more powerful and less democratic – power and democracy do not really go hand–in-hand, as is determined by the human condition and as history clearly shows. Power always corrupts us – to a greater or lesser extent.

Today (26.7.2019) once again we see the raw face of hate which has reappeared on the college campus scene. The memorial of Emmett Till was not only desecrated with bullets but three white college boys posed with guns in front of it.

- Emmett Till was a 14-year old African boy who left the safety of his parents Chicago home to visit his grandmother in Mississippi. He was warned about racism but had no idea what it really meant. It was said that he 'offended'* a white woman and so late that night he was dragged out of his bed, brutally tortured and then shot. His body was thrown in the river. His attackers were acquitted by an all-White jury. He got no justice. Now again with hate being openly espoused, what are we to expect from the free world? More hate? More racism? Are intimidation and violence back again? Does the world have to relive that terrible chapter again? It bodes ill for the future because things now aren't quite what they were in 1955. Now we do have voices that protest such behaviour.

In this book I hope to share with you my trepidation, worry and fear for the future of our world. Wherever I look, I see a dismal picture of a world in disarray – of a world in turmoil. We have betrayed our inheritance. No matter which religion or race we belong to, we are all guilty. Everywhere you look, there is murder and mayhem; there is toil and trouble; there is betrayal and death. We murder, we bear false witness, we corrupt our Holy Books – the Bible, Quran and Torah as well as Buddha's guidelines. All these Books and teachings advocate tolerance, respect for life and for other people, yet if we look at the world around us it is the opposite we see. Buddha insisted on not harming other living creatures and for example, in Buddhist Myanmar the opposite is happening - murder, rape, violence, displacement of whole communities is the order of the day, not tolerance and amity. We are the generations that are guilty of meaningless crimes. No place in the world is safe anymore and the most innocuous of places – the hearth, the home, school, church, mosque, synagogue, temple, restaurant, playground, classroom, hotel, concert hall are all death traps. At any time death may walk our way and stalk us. And we seem unable to learn the lessons of the ages – hate begets hate; murder begets revenge/murder; and most importantly – the one we should follow – love begets love or forgiveness.

Perhaps only a conflagration can purify our corrupt world.

NB
*Emmett Till supposedly whistled at a white woman.

Political Issues

The Hollow men
By <u>T.S. Eliot</u>

Eyes I dare not meet in dreams
In death's dream kingdom
These do not appear:
There the eyes are
Sunlight on a broken column...

This is dead land. This is cactus land
Here the stone images
Are raised, here they receive
The supplication of a dead man's hand
Under the twinkle of a fading star.

See yonder poor, o'er laboured wight
So abject, mean and vile
Who begs a brother of the earth
To give him leave to toil
And see his lordly fellow worm
The poor petition spurn
Unmindful that a weeping wife
And helpless offspring mourn
Man was made to Mourn by Robert Burns

Nazism in some form, going by other names has always existed. In recent years it has become more focussed, arrogant and brain-washed. For example Jews were always discriminated against in most European countries like Germany, England France etc. History tells us that. But with the twentieth century Nazis it went beyond simple hate. Hitler desired to eradicate the Jews and to that end his party forced its dogma on the nation and brain-washed them. Hate became a central dogma for the Nazi party. Hate is a very negative emotion that corrodes the soul. It has no positive value but leaders who are dictators or would be dictators promote hate. They brainwash their followers to hate some chosen part of society that they feel threatened by. World War II showed us the power of hate. It should have served as a lesson to us but once again hate has snaked into our lives.

Nazism is not dead. Far from it! It is very much alive and gaining strength. After World War II, most people believed that Nazism was over and done with. This was not the case at all. It was dormant, gathering strength and disciples not just in Germany but in many others – waiting for the correct moment to rear its head again. The difference now was that Nazism was not confined to just one country but had crept into many nations and it was not just nationalism and anti-Semitism that drove it but many other ideologies with different names. The first modern Nazi name that comes to mind is the Neo-Nazi. They hold the same basic views as the Nazis did but are also extreme nationalists, homophobic, racist, anti-Semitic and in many cases anti-Islam. Some of the most well-known groups are the Skinheads and the White Nationalists in different countries. Some European and Latin American countries have laws forbidding the use of Nazi symbols and airing of pro-Nazi views. But there too, they are present. In the US there are several neo-Nazi groups like the Nationalist Socialist Movement, the Neo Nazis, The White Supremacists, The Ku Klux Klan etc. Nazi gestures are acceptable as we saw in a recent Trump meeting where the crowd shouted – "Heil Trump" with the Nazi gesture of the outstretched arm in July 2019. It should have given us all pause for thought. And this not the first time he got the Nazi salute.

First of all let us get an idea about the ideology of the Neo-Nazis. They are a militant socio--political movement seeking to revive and implement Hitler's ideology. The modern day Neo-Nazis espouse beliefs that they are superior, hatred towards Jews, Muslims and all who are different from them in any way, like the Blacks, Hispanics and coloured people, the lesbians and homosexuals and all others. In short anyone who is not White Anglo-Saxon.

In the United States there are about 21 Neo-Nazi parties who are dominant and strong groups.

The majority of movements are to be found in the US and Germany followed by the United Kingdom. There are a few scattered over many other nations like Russia, Norway, Sweden, Belgium and the Netherlands, Denmark, Spain, Ukraine, Serbia, Croatia, Bosnia, Finland and even in Asia and Africa.

In Asia the movements are centred in Taiwan, Japan, Iran, Mongolia, Syria. These are not really as powerful as those in Europe.

In Oceania they can be found in the following countries: Australia, (4 movements) and New Zealand (1 movement).

The signs were there for those who looked for them. The stage was being readied. By the year 2000 they made their reappearance.

Neo-Nazis Today

In the US though there are many parties the membership is not as frighteningly large as that in Germany taken by the size of the land they inhabit. The largest movement is the National Socialist movement with over 400 members. Because USA is a democracy and free speech is allowed, there are peaceful protests. But there are also a lot of situations when Neo-Nazis have attacked or harassed Jews, homosexuals and minorities as well as wrecking their property.

Neo-Nazi's are more visible in Europe especially Germany where Nazi membership is over five and a half thousand and still increasing. These organisations are officially banned as is Holocaust denial but it is really only on paper. One of the main tenants of Neo-Nazism is Holocaust denial. A very large number of people believe it was a hoax. This group is almost as large as the haters. Recently Muslim haters have also become much more open, vocal and visible.

This brings me to my point: Hate. It is easy to hate anyone or anything that you do not understand or covet or are told to hate because they are different to you. Hate is wrong. Hate is a weakness. Hate begets hate. Hate is a loser.

Trump has radically changed the values we were taught to live by. He has done very poorly by the free America that he became President of. He is very intolerant of those who are different from him. He advocates and kindles the flames of hate, and racism and then denies any culpability!

Islamic Republic of Afghanistan

Man's inhumanity to man: Makes countless thousands mourn!
Robert Burns

Afghanistan is the forgotten war. Even though the killing there is going on apace, it no longer makes the front pages. These 18 long years now, the war still does not seem to be coming to an end. The might of the US is ranged against a poor, small little country. Not many even remember why it began.

This is a landlocked country lying in South and Central Asia. It is bordered by Pakistan to the south and east; by Iran to the west and Uzbekistan, Turkmenistan and Tajikistan to the North and China to the northeast. The main languages are Pashto and Dari. The religion is Muslim. The capital city and the largest is Kabul which has been heavily bombed time and time again.

Afghanistan is located very strategically and for that reason has housed many different peoples like the Hephathalites, Greco-Bactarians, the Kushans, the Samanids, the Saffrids and the Ghaznavids among others. It is often called the *graveyard of empires* because it has always been very difficult to conquer and keep. It has been invaded by many different peoples like the Greeks under Alexander the Great, The Mauryas from India, the Mongols, the Mughal Arabs, the British the Soviets and in recent times it has been the USA and the NATO coalition. The bombing and fighting are still continuing now in 2019 mainly by the USA.

After King Zahir Shah was overthrown by his brother-in-law Mohammad Daoud Shah, the country became a republic in 1978 but a second coup soon followed, and it became a Socialist state and then a Soviet Protectorate. This gave birth to the Mujahideens to fight against the Soviets and in 1996 it was taken over by the Islamic fundamentalist - the Talibans. They were forcibly removed by the

USA and NATO. This was an independent country at peace with its neighbours. It had broken no NATO rules nor had it attacked any other country. It was resolving an internal problem but as is often the case with the USA, it needed to be bombed for reasons that were fictitious – at best. The reason given was that USA had to free the country from the Talibans. Does the rest of the world need to free the USA from the Neo-Nazis?

Afghanistan is a member off The UNO and the Non-Aligned Movement (like Serbia when it was too, bombed while trying to solve an US induced internal problem). It is also a member of the *Organisation of Islamic Cooperation, The Group of 77 and the Economic Cooperation group.*

Afghanistan is very strategically located (as mentioned earlier) on the Silk Route and that is one reason why it is and was often under attack. But it is often called "unconquerable" because of its terrain which is rugged and mountainous with deep valleys and gorges. The Khyber Pass road can only be navigated by drivers experienced on that route. On one side are very high and steep mountains, and on the other side sheer drops. The road is narrow and winding

In the 1930's Afghanistan had good relations with the Axis powers but remained non-aligned and did not participate in World War II. Then, during the Cold War, both USSR and USA vied for influence. In 1978 Afghanistan descended into civil war led by the Mujahideen guerrillas, which was due to certain governmental polices including that of land reform. The USSR supported the ruling group (*The People's Democratic Party of Afghanistan the PDPA*). And as usual USA supported the anti-USSR rebel Mujahideen. Soon after, the president, Taraki was assassinated and USSR invaded Afghanistan. The USA continued to supply trained fighters, weapons, cash and air missiles to the Mujahideen. Following the subsequent breakup of the USSR it left the ruling party without any support while the rebels were still backed by the USA. The stage was set for what came after.

By 1985 they were still fighting even though the Soviet war had taken its toll and a large number of Afghanis were displaced. By 1989 the Soviets had withdrawn after about 10 years of war. The peace accords were agreed to by the USSR, USA, Afghanistan and Pakistan. Unfortunately, the country dissolved into civil war as with US interference the governing body in Afghanistan was toppled.

In 1995 the Taliban emerged as a militant Islamic group and captured many cities including Kabul, the capital in 1996 and imposed the Sharia law (similar to that in Saudi Arabia) into the state. (Note: USA has no problem whatsoever with Saudi Arabia's harsh use of the Sharia law and its dictatorial regime mainly because it is very rich and USA benefits from its cheap oil. The crown Prince of Saudi Arabia who has been involved in the Jamal Khasshogi horrible murder is a great friend of Trump's). From 1996 to 2001 the Al-Qaeda under Osama bin Laden was also operating in Afghanistan. After the assassination of Masoud on September 9, 2001 –before the twin tower bombing in New York and Washington D.C., USA demanded that Bin Laden be handed over to them as they suspected him of being behind the assassination. (Osama bin Laden was supposed to have been trained in the USA. **He was a Saudi Arabian citizen**). The Taliban replied that they would hand him over to a third country to stand trial. USA refused and began the covert CIA operation –*Jawbreaker*. About 50 countries, until now, have sent troops to fight in Afghanistan – a poor, small, third world country.

On November 14, 2001, after the fall of the Taliban in Kabul, the UN Security Council passed Resolution 1378, calling for the UN participation in forming a transitional government in Kabul. In December 2001, several Afghan leaders travelled to an UN conference in Bonn, Germany and an interim government was decided upon. What then happened that led to open warfare? In April 2002 President George W Bush said: *By helping to build an Afghanistan free from evil and a better place to live, we are working in the best traditions of George Marshall.* So, what went wrong?

Later *Operation Enduring Freedom* under the UK and US forces was openly begun in October 2001. The US and UK forces bombed the country including AL Qaeda camps. In 2011, President Barack Obama promised a gradual exit of all-American troops from Afghanistan but the troops are still there in 2019. In 2015 Obama said that due to the escalation of hostilities 8,400 troops would remain in Afghanistan for the foreseeable future till at least 2017 because he said: *We have to deal with the realities of the world.* Until now, 2019 the US still has forces in Afghanistan and the killing is still going on. Had both the USSR and USA not interfered in the internal problems of Afghanistan, there would have been peace in that country and a lot of lives, both coalition and Afghani, would have been saved.

The main reason what the USA gave for attacking Afghanistan was that it was to take out the Al Qaida who, they 'said', was behind the September 11, 2001 attack on the towers of New York and Washington D.C. This has never been proven, though it has been said that the Al Qaida was not the culprit in the attack on the towers in the USA **(CF Farenheight 11** by Michael Moore – a political documentary – DVD).** The then US President, George W Bush vowed *to win the war against terrorism.* Wouldn't it have been better to fight terrorism on the home front instead of going across the continents to attack a small foreign country? It was decided that it would be an US led coalition against the Taliban and Al Qaida. The coalition expected it to be a short affair but now in 2019, after 18 years, it is still going on and people are dying for nothing! To the leader (leading country) of the free world, interfering in the freedom of another country is acceptable!

The Taliban denied being guilty of the attack on the USA and refused to hand over Al Qaeda leaders and especially Osama bin Laden, its chief leader. On September 18, 2001 President Bush signed a resolution allowing for the use of force against Afghanistan. Later this resolution was quoted as giving the US the right to eavesdrop in on private conversations of private Americans and for the establishment of a terrible detention camp (a prison) in Guatanamo Bay. It is still regarded as one of the worst and most inhumane 'detentation' centres in the world. On October 7, 2001 The US-led coalition *Enduring Freedom* attacked Afghanistan. US bases were set up near most major Afghan cities. The Northern Alliance – an Afghan group who were against the Taliban joined with the US. Few of the Taliban or Al Qaeda were captured or killed. They had escaped to the mountains and to the rugged and inaccessible interior of the country.

Britain and the US bombed the country while others – France, Canada, Germany and Australia promised to help later. On November 14, 2001, after the fall of the Taliban the UN Security Council passed Resolution 1378 allowing for the UN participation in a transitional government in Afghanistan but the fighting is still continuing now in 2019. The country is in dire straits especially economically. Medical supplies too are hard to come by. Basic amenities are severely lacking.

Afghanistan is a major hot spot and killing is still going on there. Peace is nowhere near happening. It is a country in severe turmoil. Thanks to the US, UK and USSR decision to interfere.

- According to Peyton Jacobsen *Since the beginning of the conflict, more than four dozen countries have contributed troops to the NATO-led International Security Assistance Force in Afghanistan*
- *As of 2015, the U.S. committed **over $685 billion** to funding the war in Afghanistan. Along with the Iraq War, the Afghanistan War has been the most expensive in U.S. history.*

Osama bin Laden was killed in Pakistan on May 2, 2011 by US Navy Seals called Naval Special Warfare Development Group or DEVGRU or SEAL Team of Six.

Can storied urn or animated bust
Back to its mansion call the fleeting breath?
Can honour's voice provoke the silent dust,
Or Flattery soothe the dull cold ear of death?
        Elegy written in a Country Churchyard – Thomas Gray

Iraq is a country in Southwestern Asia. It is bordered to the north by Turkey, Saudi Arabia to the South, Kuwait to the Southeast, Jordan to the Southwest, Iran to the East and Syria to the West. The capital and largest city is Baghdad. There are many ethnic groups living there.

Iraq is a very old civilization. It was the seat of many great civilizations like the Babylonians, Assyrians, Sumerians, Hellenistic, Roman, Abbasid and Ottoman among many others. It was the place where reading, writing and the first code of laws (*Hammurabi's Code of Law*) began. It is regarded as the Cradle of civilization. Its old name was Mesopotamia – the land between the Tigris and Euphrates Rivers or the Fertile Crescent.

The present-day name Iraq comes from the word Uruk after the name of the ancient city of Uruk. It came under British rule in 1920 when the British established it as the Hashemite Kingdom under King Faisal I. After it had sided with Germany in World War I and was defeated it then came under British rule again. It gained independence from Britain in 1932 and the Monarchy was overthrown in 1958 when it became a Republic.

In 1958 there was a revolution under Qasim. In 1968 the Ba'ath party came to power following another Revolution with Abu Bakr as the president and Saddam Hussein the vice president. In 1968 Abu-Bakr resigned and Saddam became the president in 1979. Under him the country became strong and rich by exporting oil. There were no beggars or homeless people. Hospitals and schools were very good.

Iraq had huge oil reserves and so the economy was good. The country was very prosperous.

In 1980 Iraq declared war on Iran following the coup in Iran and the establishment of the Ayatollah Khomeni and the Islamic Republic in Iran. This war depleted Iraqi resources and it led to a ceasefire.

Saddam modernised Iraq. He modernised the economy, the security system especially around himself to prevent any coup from taking place from within and to control insurrections from taking place too – Iraq being the home of different ethnic groups and different religious sects. He widened his base to include diverse peoples and mobilized mass support. He took an active interest in the functioning of the administration, state welfare and development programmes.

At the heart of all this was oil. In June 1972, he seized all international oil interests in Iraq as oil was the most important commodity that they had. In 1973 oil prices skyrocketed and this enabled Saddam to expand his agendas.

Soon he had an excellent welfare system in place, unprecedented in the Middle-East. Some things he did was establish the *National Campaign for the Eradication of Illiteracy, Compulsory Free Education in Iraq;* he also established free schooling for the highest education, government support for families of soldiers, free medical treatment for all, and gave subsidies to farmers, among other things. He truly created a very modern health care system in Iraq for which Iraq was given an award from UNESCO.

Saddam now decided to diversify the mainly oil-based economy of Iraq. With good revenue coming in from oil, Saddam was able to invest more in the infrastructure of the country. Now electricity was available in almost every city and suburb. New wider roads were constructed, irrigation systems were established both in the north and south of the country, telephone lines were laid. Communication was much easier. More and more people started moving from villages and farms to cities. Industrial expansion began on a major scale.

With the end of the Iraq-Iran war, relations between Iraq and Kuwait deteriorated. Saddam asked Kuwait to waive the debt Iraq had accrued during the Iraq-Iran war. Kuwait refused. And when Iraq asked the oil-producing countries to raise the oil price, – again Kuwait refused. Instead Kuwait took the lead to oppose Saddam with OPEC by keeping prices low when Iraq needed that money in its rebuilding process.

With US foreknowledge (Cf. *Carnage by Appointment* by Maria Seferou) Iraq attacked Kuwait and then in August 6, 1990 The Gulf War began. Iraq soon faced a coalition of 30 nations led by the USA and mandated by the UN ostensibly to liberate Kuwait. In actual fact it was to curb Iraq's power and make sure it did not control the Kuwaiti and Saudi Arab oilfields because that would give it too much power. Moreover, Kuwait was the US supplier of oil. *Operation Desert Storm* began ostensibly to free Kuwait and protect Saudi Arabia – another oil supplier to the US!!

The Iraqis had no chance against the coalition (USA and NATO even though no NATO country was attacked by Iraq) with their fresh soldiers, huge armies and the latest weapons. In 1991 Iraq was defeated but the US set up a base in Iraq which is still there - now ostensibly to fight ISIS. Very stringent sanctions were imposed on Iraq. The number of Iraqi soldiers killed has been very modestly put down to 85,000 at the end of the war and 175,000 were captured.

Until now soldiers and civilians are still dying in Iraq, bombs are exploding, medicines are difficult to come by, people are starving. The coalition soldiers are also dying. So what is the point in war??? No one really wins. In this case, I agree with Trump in wanting to bring back US soldiers and save their lives.

Gulf War from August 1990 to 1991 brought about another face of war where large coalitions band together to destroy smaller much weaker countries – but countries that are either rich in oil like, Iraq, Libya or are strategically located like Afghanistan Serbia.

Then in March 2003, a UN organised coalition using the pretext that Iraq had violated UN Resolution 687 and had not abandoned its weapons of mass destruction again invaded Iraq in force. No such weapons were found. CIA had provided the documents to the UN for this. US President George W Bush said: *The Iraqi regime has plotted to develop anthrax, and nerve gas, and nuclear weapons for over a decade ... Iraq continues to flaunt its hostility toward America and to support terror.* And in his State of the Union Address he talked about an *axis of evil* consisting of Iran, North Korea and Iraq.

After the attack of 9/11 President Bush's administrations began planning the overthrow of Saddam Hussein's government in October 2002. In November UNSCR passed Resolution 1441 and in March 2003 USA and its allies invaded Iraq.

The United Nations Security Council Resolution 1441 demanded Iraq give unconditional and immediate cooperation and they also put very harsh sanctions on Iraq, sanctions that remained in place till May 2003. No weapons of mass destruction or chemical weapons were ever found in Iraq – the reason for attacking Iraq in the first place. It was a trumped-up charge.

Within three weeks the Iraqi government collapsed. On 13 December *Operation Red Dawn* began. Saddam was captured and taken to an American Base near Baghdad. He was hanged in 2006 on the Muslim feast day. He had requested to be executed by a firing squad as being a military man but was refused.

There is still no peace in Iraq today in 2019. The ravages of war are apparent everywhere. Bombs are still exploding, people are still being killed. There is death and disease around every corner of the country. Children are dying at a frightening rate. There is a huge refugee crises and crippling sectarianism.

In the past decade, Iraqis have made some progress in building their government—approving a constitution to replace that of the Saddam Hussein era, and holding successive elections for parliament and provincial governments. Still, governing institutions remain weak, and corruption and poverty endemic.

In 2014 after ISIS seized parts of northwestern Iraq and adjacent parts of Syria, US again returned to Iraq in force. Time only will tell how this plays out.

The Kosovo Problem – The Aftermath

In 1992-3 The NATO with strong US demands decided to attack The Federal Republic of Yugoslavia (FRY) and break it up into many small states. To understand why this was so and why it was necessary, we need to go back in time.

During World War II the Croatians who were part of the Austro-Hungarian Empire and who, it appeared, had a grudge against the Serbs wiped out one third of the Serb population in the concentration camp of Jasenovac. After the war Marshall Tito, with strong UK support and against Mikhailović – a Serb patriot combined the states of Serbia, Croatia, Bosnia-Herzegovina, Slovenia, Macedonia Montenegro and the Serbian provinces of Vojvodina and Kosovo and Metohija into the FRY. Kosovo since ages past has been Serbian territory. Pristina, the largest city - now capital of Kosovo, was the capital of the Kingdom of Serbia long before FRY was formed. But under Tito things began to change. He displaced 100,000 Serbs from Kosovo and invited Albanians from Albania to come down from their barren hills and take over the Serb dwellings. That is how the Albanians came to a Serbian heartland.

FRY was a model social welfare state. There were no beggars or homeless people. Medical treatment was free as was Primary and Secondary education. Kindergartens were also free. It appears that this irked some.

In 1991 President George Bush forced through Congress a bill called the *Foreign Appropriations Bill 101-513*, which was announced in May by the then Secretary of State, James Baker. Briefly this bill meant FRY had no authority over FRY (See Document A, Appendix 1). It was up to the United States to decide FRY's internal affairs – as happened in South and Central America, in Vietnam and Korea and in more recent time in the Middle East and Afghanistan and to an extent in the USSR which too was broken up and dismantled.

All the different states of the FRY except for Serbia were offered all kinds of help if they would break away from Serbia. And so it happened. Problems began with Bosnia-Herzegovina and Croatia. With US-NATO help both broke away from the FRY after a lot of bloodshed. Then the US decided it was time to create a new state in Kosovo and give the Albanians a new state. The reason I believe is the following:

US needed a base in Southern Europe. Now they have Bondsteel Base under KFOR command since 1999 – the largest US military base in Europe. They show no signs of going back to their homes. And in Kosovo they certainly are not protecting the Serbs who are being murdered by the Kosovo Albanians. Almost every day one hears about some new attack on the Serbs of Kosovo. Now the US no longer calls it ethnic cleansing (Cf. Betrayal – a political documentary by Ashley Smith) or calls for NATO to intervene. KFOR troops patrol Kosovo but don't see anything. This is called convenient blindness. It was never about their great love for the Kosovo Muslim Albanians. It was to establish a base there. Now Muslims are anathema to Trump and his henchmen and Trump would have them barred from going to the US at all – if he could do so. However the Saudi Muslims and the Kosovo Muslims are buddies and he will not even accept that Crown Prince Mohammad Bin Salam ordered or at least had a hand in the Khashoggi murder in spite of the evidence available. Kosovo, it appears is set to be a world hot spot now and in the near future.

> *Their lot forbade: nor circumscribed alone*
> *Their growing virtues, but their crimes confined;*
> *Forbade to wade through slaughter to a throne,*
> *And shut the gates of mercy on mankind.*
> *Elegy written in a Country Churchyard* by
> Thomas Gray

Haiti and Honduras are small, poor countries with little in the way of resources, so why should US be interested in having influence there? But they do - enough to have overthrown the elected president Jean Bertrand Aristide twice – in1991 and in 2004 because he was again democratically elected. There is ample proof that the CIA was involved both times in overthrowing him - though in 1991 it was more covert. In fact Emmanuel Constant, leader of the most notorious death squad that killed thousands of supporters of Aristide, himself said that he was funded by the CIA to do so. On the one hand US told Aristide to compromise with the opposition and on the other hand dissuaded the opposition from doing so and instead funded the opposition with millions of US dollars.

This was not the first time that the USA had interfered in **Haitian** affairs. In 1915 the US acquired the National Bank of Haiti to circumvent and nullify German influence. But after two decades of dictatorial rule by the US-friendly Vilbrun Guillaume Sam, he (and his government) was overthrown. US Sent in the Marines to occupy Haiti which they did. The US wielded the power to veto any government decision there. It also administered the country through US Marines as regional administrators. But when the Marines withdrew US-backed military dictatorships took its place for the next 50 years especially under the dictator François Duvalier, also known as Papa Doc or Doc Duvallier (Daddy Doc), who was the President of Haiti from 1957 to 1971. He was elected president in

1957 on a populist and Black Nationalist platform. After thwarting a military coup d'état in 1958, his regime rapidly became totalitarian and despotic. An undercover government death squad, the Tonton Macoute, killed opponents indiscriminately, and was thought to be so pervasive that Haitians became highly fearful of expressing dissent, even in private. Papa Doc was fully supported by the US.

In 2010 in **Honduras**, under Obama the US government did all it could to support the coup government from being penalised. It successfully blocked other American states from supporting the elected government and not the coup dictatorship. All the while the Obama government falsely proclaimed its opposition to the coup.

In **Brazil** in 1964 There was a serious coup d'état against several decades of US backed dictatorial governments. Joäo Goulart had come to power with American backing. John F Kennedy had said, this was to prevent Brazil from becoming another Cuba. However, Brazil did manage to return to democracy but its economy was shattered. In 2005 US intervened openly in their election process. First of all, they (US) organised a conference to promote a change of government. This is because the US did not like Lula's democratically elected party. This information only came to light in 2009.

The US government has also been heavily involved in manipulating parties and they were directly involved in overthrowing the democratically elected **Chilean** democracy of Salvador Allende in 1973. He was replaced by the US choice of the brutal dictator Augusto Pinochet. Since then it has mostly been right-wing US supported parties in power in Chile. Pinochet was finally democratically removed by the *Concertation of Parties for Democracy*. They ruled except for 2 periods.

Though there is controversy surrounding the 1973 **Chilean** coup even today, there is certainly evidence of communication between the CIA and the coup instigators led by Gen. Augusto Pinochet.

Salvador Allende was a democratically elected president with ties to Cuba's Fidel Castro. In September 1973, he was overthrown by a military junta. The CIA was aware of the coup as many as two days in advance. Following the event, in a conference with President Nixon, National Security Adviser Henry Kissinger stated that *"the Chilean thing is getting consolidated and of course the newspapers are bleeding because a pro-Communist government has been overthrown."* Pinochet's regime went on to become one of the most oppressive and brutal organizations of the 20th Century.

Finally in 2006, Michelle Bachelet was elected as the President. Her father was always loyal to Allende, for which reason both he and his daughter were arrested and tortured during Pinochet's time. After his (Pinochet's) removal from office, a lot of corruption scandals about Pinochet came to light.

Panama used to be a part of Colombia following its independence from Spain. The Colombian government had negotiated with the US to build a canal to bridge the Atlantic and Pacific oceans, but the deal fell through and a separatist movement in Panama ensued which the US supported. After the establishment of the Republic of Panama, the French engineering magnate Philip Burnau-Varilla sold his concession to the building rights for the canal to the US government. The US demanded control of the canal and the six-mile zone around it. The tension culminated in the 1964 riots that killed 22 Panamanians and 4 US soldiers. Control of the Canal was then transferred back to Panama in 1999 after the President, Omar Torrijo's plane crashed killing him and leaving the way open for the American backed Manuel Noriega. However soon afterwards their relationship deteriorated and the Americans invaded Panama. After this the then US President Teddy Roosevelt announced his corollary to the previous *Monroe Doctrine*, (See Annex B) stating that the US could act unilaterally to ward off European intervention in the Caribbean because he wanted to protect his investment in Panama. He obtained the rights to administer the Dominican customs, its chief source of income. Under President Obama the policy of supporting rightwing governments in Panama and Colombia continued and they in turn supported Obama's policies in Latin and Central America.

Then, in 1916, the US invaded and established a military government under Admiral Knapp, which was rejected by the **Dominicans.** This government was often brutal in its crackdown on dissent. The US occupation did not end until 1922. The Dominican Republic was considered a protectorate of the US until 1941.

The US Marines were sent to occupy **Nicaragu**a beginning in 1912 in the midst of an armed insurrection. The US was also granted rights to build a so-called "Nicaragua Canal" by the conservative US-backed Chamorro ruling family. Later, Gen. Augusto Sandino led a rebellion against the conservative government and US occupation. Sandino was later assassinated, and the military dictatorship of the Somoza family came into power. This too was backed by the US-trained Guardia Nacional. (Cf. *Betrayal a Political Documentary* by Ashley Smith).

Following guerilla leader Pancho Villa's raid on Columbus, **New Mexico** (in which 16 Americans died), President Wilson sent Gen. "Blackjack" Pershing and 10,000 soldiers into the mountains of northern Mexico to hunt Villa down. The mission ultimately failed but Mexicans viewed the act as an unjust invasion. It has been an uneasy relationship since then.

> *US & the Mexican Border*
> *At the margins of the mainstream discursive stalemate*
> *over immigration lies over a century of historical*
> *U.S. intervention that politicians and pundits on both*
> *sides of the aisle seem determined to silence. Since*
> *Theodore Roosevelt in 1904 declared the U.S.'s right*
> *to exercise an "international police power" in Latin*
> *America, the U.S. has cut deep wounds throughout the*

region, leaving scars that will last for generations to come. This history of intervention is inextricable from the contemporary Central American crisis of internal and international displacement and migration.

Mark Tseng -Putterma

In the early 1950s, the Central Intelligence Agency (CIA) organized a coup against the democratically elected President Arbenz in **Guatemala**. Arbenz had instituted sweeping land reforms to benefit the country's vast impoverished populace. This antagonized the powerful United Fruit Company, a multi-national conglomerate, of which CIA director Allen Dulles was a stockholder, and which lobbied the US government for intervention. The moves were also deemed Communist in nature by the Eisenhower administration and the US government began to supply anti-Arbenz forces with weapons and training. Arbenz was overthrown, and military dictatorship followed for the next four decades. During this time, it is estimated that nearly a quarter million Guatemalans were killed or "disappeared."

US President Eisenhower oversaw plans to depose Communist **Cuban** leader Fidel Castro as early as 1960, using much the same model as the one used in Guatemala. Castro had deposed the US-backed Batista regime in the Revolution, and had since developed close ties with the Soviet Union. The plans came to fruition under the Kennedy administration. A force of anti-Castro Cuban exiles was landed in Southern Cuba (Bay of Pigs) on April 17, 1961, supported by strikes on Cuban airfields. By this time, however, Castro's forces were well equipped with advanced Soviet weapons and the invasion was defeated. Tensions between the US and Cuba would be strained to a breaking point with the Cuban Missile Crisis the following year.

The Platt Amendment
1901

This addition to the Army Appropriations Act, submitted by Senator Orville Platt (R-Ohio), set the stage for US-Cuban relations in the early 20th Century. Following the war with Spain in 1898, the US maintained a large garrison in Cuba in the interest of creating a self-governing colony **subordinate** to Washington. The terms of the amendment included

1. restriction of land leasing to any nation but the US,
2. ensuring of US intervention in Cuban affairs and

3. prohibition of negotiating treaties with any power other than the US.

The amendment also provided the framework for the leasing of Guantanamo Bay to US control, which became an even more divisive issue upon transfer of detainees to the area following the September 11 attacks and subsequent wars. The Guantanamo Prison was established with Guantanamo Naval Base in January 2002 by the Bush administration to ostensibly house dangerous prisoners. It has been condemned as a very inhumane prison.

Grenada is a small Caribbean island about 100 miles north of Venezuela. In 1979, a revolution led by Maurice Bishop came to power with Cuban support. Among his projects was the construction of a large airstrip, which was charged by US President Reagan as designed for Soviet aircraft. An internal power struggle followed, ending in Bishop's arrest and execution. At the time, 800 US medical students were on the island, and their presence amid the turmoil gave Reagan sufficient justification for ordering an invasion. Ten thousand US, Jamaican and Caribbean troops landed on Oct. 25, 1983. The invasion was condemned internationally by the UN General Assembly. Twenty American troops were killed, along with over a hundred Cuban and Grenadian soldiers and civilians.

In **Argentina,** the democratic Isabel Perón was overthrown in 1976 in a coup d état. The US-backed military dictator Jorge Rafael Videla came to power. Over 30,000 victims went missing in what was termed the *National Reorganization Process.* The US and Henry Kissenger strongly endorsed him including in his human rights violations, rapes, mass executions, extrajudicial arrests etc. (Judge Baltazar Garzon - Spanish).

In 1983 Raul Alfonso won the votes putting an end to the military junta. However, the 1998-2002 great depression caused great upheaval and a number of presidents came and went.

In **Peru,** the US sponsored government of Alberto Fujimorei and Vladimiro Montesinos came to power. They were extremely corrupt, and this finally led to their downfall. A few democratic governments followed. Peru stayed on as a part of the Pacific Alliance.

Uruguay had 150 years of right-wing traditional government but following the coup d'etat of 1973, the US-backed Civic military dictatorship came to power. President Juan Maria Bordaberry took on dictatorial powers. He had trade union leaders, political opponents and any who opposed him arrested, exiled, killed or they just disappeared. In 1984 democracy finally was re-established under Tabare Vazquez. He was succeeded by another democrat, Jose Mujica. Vazquez was re-elected in 2014.

USA **never supports** any elected democratic governments around the world. It supports right wing parties that are weak towards the USA, despotic monarchies and dictatorships (Cf. present day Saudi Arabia, T Duarte in the Philippines, The Contras in Nicaragua, besides interfering in Paraguay in support of the dictator Stroessner, in Panama in 1991 and the list goes on. US has and is still constantly fomenting trouble in the countries not only of Central and Latin America but also in the Middle East and other parts of Asia). In its wake it brings dissension, divisiveness, destruction and death.

The political strategy of the US is always to support dictatorial regimes that go with US wishes and never the democratic, elected regime of any country. It is also the US policy to sow discord and division in other countries perhaps so as to sell arms to them and in this way they have a healthy US economy. Another thing that I see is that US usually tries to make sure of US influence and not Russian influence.

Another result of US interference in its neighbours lives is that of massive influx of asylum seekers to the US from their countries as all of the countries mentioned above have been recipients of US 'kindness' in the form of destabilising their nations and creating discord.

But now President Trump calls them (asylum seekers) murderers and what-not. He has adopted a "zero-tolerance policy' towards them. Children are ripped from their parents and caged in enclosures. Trump has signed an executive order that is to keep families at the border - separated. Mass detention and mass deportation are the order of the day! God help us all!!

US political strategy stays the same no matter which party or person is in power especially when it concerns US influence. Countries closer to the US are of course much more at risk like the Latin American, Central American and South American states. And they have all paid with the blood of their innocents for that proximity.

First of all the US under successive administrations has turned the Central Americas into a hell hole and now when civilians are trying to escape from murder, mayhem, gun violence and gang violence, the Trump administration has closed the borders already or are in the process of doing so; are building a wall and to add insult to injury are saying that these civilians including children are gang members. They are being put in cages and not given any proper care.

Immigration has always been a very controversial issue in US politics. In the last few years it has worsened. Under Obama 2.5 million immigrants (Justin Sybenga) were deported but since Donald Trump's presidency it has reached huge proportions. Trump is obsessed with building a border wall whether it will serve the purpose or not. He has also racially targeted the asylum seekers calling them all *criminals, the brown horde and rats*, hoping that the wall will keep them out. This has further exacerbated the situation. Children have died in Border Patrol custody – through no fault of theirs but because of the unmanageable number of applicants and lack of facilities. In September 2017 Trump rescinded the DACA (Deferred Action for Childhood Arrivals) programme. This too put much more pressure on the border patrols and ended the temporary relief of deportation for them. Then the Homeland Security announced that it would not be renewing the Temporary Protected Status designation of refugees from many countries hit by natural disasters or military conflicts. All this is adding to an already volatile situation. Trump also believes that most people who seek asylum are in fact criminals. This is simply not true.

> *This is the dead land*
> *This is cactus land....*
> *In this valley of dying stars*
> *In this hollow valley*
> *This broken jaw of our lost kingdom*
> *We grope together...*
>
> *The Hollow Men –* **Thomas Stearns Eliot**

Like Afghanistan and Iraq, Libya too was a recipient of US and NATO kindness - bombs and interference. But here the hypocrisy of the administration was more exposed. There was an internal problem going on in Libya when the UN under the goading from The US decided to interfere in Libya's internal problems by ostensibly saying that the US-NATO troops were there to have a no-fly zone and no support was to be given to either side. In actual fact, according to those involved in the active commission of their duty, it was to support the rebels and take down President Muammar Gaddafi. Gaddafi's residential area was bombed, rebels were allowed to bring in arms and were also given air cover. All the while US - NATO denied any involvement to take out Gaddafi.

Security Council Resolution 1970

In contemporary political debates, the Libya intervention tends to be remembered as an intra-administration soap opera, focused on the role Clinton — or Susan Rice or Samantha Power — played in advising Obama to go through with it. Or it is addressed offhandedly in reference to the 2012 terrorist attacks on the U.S. special mission and CIA annex in Benghazi. But it would be far more pertinent to treat Libya as a case study for the ways that supposedly limited interventions tend to mushroom into campaigns for regime change.

Five years on, it's still not a matter of public record when exactly Western powers decided to topple Qaddafi. (Wikipedia)

The Libyan crises spun out of control in 2011 when UK, US and France interfered in Libya and bombed the government forces while simultaneously giving logistic aid to the rebels. As a result, a prolonged civil war resulted. The NATO action was wrong and flawed from the start and the adoption of *Security Council Resolution 1973* should never have been adopted. The Resolution authorised *the use of all necessary measures to protect Libyan civilians and civilian-populated areas.* This did not happen because all areas under government control were bombed.

According to Dr. Laaroussi, Resolution 1973 *confirm[ed] the intention of the United States to seek an international mandate for the use of force and show[ed] the Council's willingness to apply the doctrine of the responsibility to protect".* This is borne out by the subsequent actions of the US-NATO group. A secret report picked up by Sputnik (by В. Кузнецов) says: *The significance of the US move to [gain] international legitimacy should not be exaggerated",* the academic pointed out. *"Moreover, the intervention developments in Libya have done more to discredit the concept of the 'responsibility to protect' than any criticism from an international law perspective possibly could. Libya has become a [failed] state and a 'black hole' for terrorists, arms trafficking and illegal migrant flows.*

Given this, it is hardly surprising that *"Russia and China are no longer willing to grant NATO states a mandate for action",* the professor added.

On March 28, 2011, U.S. President Barack Obama addressed the nation saying: *The task that I assigned our forces [is] to protect the Libyan people from immediate danger and to establish a no-fly zone.... Broadening our military mission to include regime change would be a mistake.* Two days later, Assistant Secretary of State

Philip Gordon announced: *The military mission of the United States is designed to implement the Security Council resolution, no more and no less.... I mean protecting civilians against attacks from Qaddafi's forces and delivering humanitarian aid."* The following day, Clinton's deputy, James Steinberg, said during a Senate hearing, *President Obama has been equally firm that our military operation has a narrowly defined mission that does not include regime change.*

In her memoir, Hilary Clinton wrote: *It's crucial we're all on the same page on NATO's responsibility to enforce the no-fly zone and protect civilians in Libya.*

US Defence Secretary Robert Gates said: *I can't recall any specific decision that said, 'Well, let's just take him out.*

If that is so, why was he taken out and who commanded it? Someone must have decided and passed it on to others. And it had to have been someone with clout. No ordinary soldier would have dared to do so otherwise and if he had taken such a decision on his own initiative, he would have got court martialled at the least.

Vice Adm. William Gortney, director of the Joint Staff when asked by the press if Gaddafi was the target, answered: *At this particular point, I can guarantee that he's not on a targeting list.* When it was then pointed out that it was Qaddafi's personal residence that had been attacked, Gortney added: *Yeah. But, no, we're not targeting his residence. We're there to set the conditions and enforce the United Nations Security Council resolution. That's what we're doing right now and limiting it to that.*

In truth, the Libyan intervention was about regime change from the very start. In fact I believe once Saddam Hussein's power was destroyed and Saddam captured, it was about disabling and destroying Gaddafi. After all, Libya had so much oil just waiting to fall into US-NATO hands.

On 19 March 2011, a multi-state <u>NATO</u>-led coalition began a military intervention in Libya, ostensibly to implement **United Nations Security Council Resolution 1973.**

The official names for the interventions by the coalition members are <u>Opération Harmattan</u> by France; <u>Operation Ellamy</u> by the United Kingdom; <u>Operation Mobile</u> for the Canadian participation and <u>Operation Odyssey Dawn</u> for the United States *"Gunfire, Explosions Heard in Tripoli". CNN. 21 March 2011. Archived from the original on 3 November 2012.*

At a congressional hearing, United States Secretary of Defense Robert Gates explained that a *no-fly zone begins with an attack on Libya to destroy the air defences ... and then you can fly planes around the country and not worry about our guys being shot down. But that's the way it starts. "U.S. Mulling Military Options in Libya".*

Operation names

Before NATO took full command of operations at 06:00 GMT on 31 March 2011, the military intervention was divided as a no-fly zone and naval blockade among different national operations under different names:

- NATO: **Operation Unified Protector**
- France: **Opération Harmattan**
- United Kingdom: **Operation Ellamy**
- Canada: **Operation Mobile**
- United States: **Operation Odyssey Dawn** – Belgium, Denmark, Italy, the Netherlands, Norway, Qatar, Spain, Greece and the United Arab Emirates placed their national contributions under US command.

The strange thing is what they said and what they did was at odds throughout the campaign. Misinformation to the public was the order of the day. Gaddafi (and his regime) was the target from the beginning. This, in my opinion was because Libya had huge reserves of oil, gold and a strong economy. He was well-liked and respected. When I travelled there in 1979, I never heard anything derogatory said about him. He walked among the populace without fearing them. So, it is hard to see how the rebellion started except through external interference.

Muammar Gaddafi, the deposed leader of Libya, was captured and killed on 20 October 2011 during the Battle of Sirte. Gaddafi was found hiding in a culvert west of Sirte and captured by National Transitional Council forces. He was killed shortly afterwards. The NTC initially claimed he died from injuries sustained in a firefight when loyalist forces attempted to free him, although a graphic video of his last moments show rebel fighters beating him and one of them sodomizing him with a bayonet before he was shot several time. (M Chulov). It was murder.

Since Gaddafi's murder, the situation in Libya has worsened vastly as different factions fight for control. The economy is shattered. Politically, to put it mildly – it is bloody and chaotic as General Khalifa Haftar tries to force a military solution.

Haftar has consolidated his position in the eastern and southern end of the country with his capital in Benghazi, while Fayez Al-Sarraj, the recognised Prime Minister heads the government in Tripoli. However, there is trouble now around Tripoli as Haftar pursues his assault on Tripoli. He is supported by UAE and Egypt. And he has already taken the oil-rich coastal region. Hafter is strong while Farraj is weak. The UN, EU and US have warned Haftar but it appears to be empty words and they too would prefer him to the in-fighting of many factions that is presently going on. USA is yet to decide how much of involvement it desires at this point in time. But it should not be forgotten that it was US interference that led to this point. Essam Omran Al-Feton said: *After the collapse of the [Muammar] Gaddafi regime, Washington has influenced, excessively, along with other regional actors, the Libyan crisis in terms of spreading the chaos in the North African region, admitting the proxy war game in this very sensitive region," the professor emphasised.*

Instead of criticising Field Marshal Khalifa Haftar, the Trump administration should encourage the political consensus between warring parties in Libya, as the US bears a great deal of responsibility for the ongoing crisis in the country. Dr. Mohammed Issam Laaroussi, professor of international relations, told Sputnik.

At the moment Britain, France and Italy have not blamed Haftar but merely asked: *all parties to restore calm.*

Palestine and the Gaza

The boast of heraldry, the pomp of power
And all that beauty, all that wealth e'er gave
Awaits alike the inevitable hour
The paths of glory lead but to the grave
    Elegy written in a country churchyard by
    Thomas Gray

Palestine (including the Gaza) was part of the Ottoman Empire before it was occupied by the UK between 1918 and 1948. Then when the Jews from the German concentration camps were freed, they were armed and settled in Palestine by the UK, France and US. Gaza was part of Egypt from 1948 to 1967. Since then, it is a very troubled spot. There is no peace there.

Palestine has a very old history. The earliest mention is in the Bronze Age when it served as an Egyptian administrative centre. The Philistines mentioned in the Bible were located here. In 332 BC it was conquered by Alexander the Great. Then it passed to the Ptolemaic dynasty followed by the Seleucids in 200 BC. The Hasmonean king, Alexander Jannaseus destroyed the city of Gaza in 96 BC. The Romans re-established it. Following the Romans it was occupied by the Persian and then the Rashidun Caliphate in the 7th century during the great Islamic expansion. The Crusades found the city more or less abandoned and it then passed to the Knight Templars. During the 12th century it passed from Muslim to Christian hands and vice versa until it passed permanently to the Muslims under the Ayubbids. It was destroyed by the Mongol Hulagu Khan. The Mamluks then re-established it until the 16th century when the Ottoman Empire took control of it. Following World War I, it passed onto the British Empire as the Mandate of Palestine following the collapse of the Ottoman Empire. This was contained in in the *San Remo Resolution of 1920 incorporating Article 22 of the Covenant of the League of Nations as well as incorporating the Balfour declaration of 1917.*

In the Arab-Israeli war of 1948, Israel invaded and captured the Gaza. At this time the All Palestinian Government was proclaimed by the Arab League in Egyptian-held Gaza, in order to limit Transjordan's influence on Palestine. Six of the seven members confirmed it – Egypt, Syria, Lebanon, Iraq, Saudi Arabia and Yemen. Transjordan refused.

At this time the refugees expelled from Palestine by Israel– 200,000 of them also settled in the Gaza. There was a dramatic worsening of living conditions. Help was given them by UNWRA. Israel called it the War of Independence while the Palestinians referred to it as Nakbah or Al Nakbah (the Catastrophe because of the many displaced refugees).

When hostilities ceased, Egypt and Israel drew up borders and established what became the now boundary line between the Gaza Strip and Israel. The southern border with Egypt stayed the same as it was under the Ottomans.

In 1956 during the Suez Canal Crises, Israel seized the Gaza Strip and the Sinai Peninsula. Under international pressure, Israel withdrew from there. In 1959 it was dissolved by a decree of the then Egyptian President Gamal Abdul Nasser. Egypt continued to occupy the Gaza Strip until 1967.

In 1967 Israel invaded the Gaza in the six-day war and at the conclusion of that fight with Egypt, occupied the Gaza Strip. In 1994 Israel granted the Palestinians of the Gaza Strip limited self-governance according to the Oslo Accord. In 2005, Israel withdrew from the Gaza Strip under the Egypt-Israel unilateral disengagement plan.

The first Israeli settlement bloc in the Gaza strip was created after the 1967 war. Between 1967 and 2005 Israel established 21 settlements in the Gaza strip. These settlements comprised 20% of the total area of the strip. The Palestinians were even more crowded. The UN did not condemn this move and neither did any Western democracy. No UN Security Council Resolution was passed. No NATO intervention took place. The best lands were taken over by the Israelis. One third of the arable strip was also taken over by the Israelis. New taxes were levied on the Palestinians and they were not allowed to trade freely. Life for the Palestinians became even more difficult and water became still more scarce. This was according to a suggestion from the then Israeli Prime Minister Levi Eshkol that restricting their water supply would force many Palestinians to leave. Eshkoff had said: *Perhaps if we don't give them enough water they won't have a choice, because the orchards will yellow and wither.* And so it happened.

In February 2005, the Jewish Knesset approved a unilateral disengagement plan by which Israeli settlers from the Gaza Strip were to be removed. And in September 12, 2005 Israel formally declared an end to Israeli occupation of the Gaza. In 2019 The US President Donald Trump gave back the Gaza Strip to Israel. Israeli settlement of the Strip began anew and so did the displacement of the Palestinians. Gaza was not Trump's to give or not give. Tom Segney says: *it was always the Israeli goal to remove or force The Palestinians out of Palestine and the Gaza since 1967.*

Since 2007 it was governed by Hamas which is considered as the Palestinian representative authority after they expelled the rival Al Fatah party. This is *de-facto* rule. However, Israel maintains indirect control even within the Gaza – it controls the air and maritime space, six of the seven crossings in the Gaza and direct external control. Israel reserves the right to enter the Gaza with its military without notice and also maintains a no-go buffer zone within the Strip. It also controls all utilities including water, electricity and telecommunications. The only border Israel does not control is the border with Egypt. According to Nissenbaum: *Since Hamas took control of Gaza last year, Israel has dramatically reduced the amount of food, fuel and supplies going through its border crossings with Gaza that are the main Palestinian lifeline to the outside world. Since the Israeli military operation on 4 November, according to humanitarian groups, about 700 truck-loads of goods have gone into Gaza. That's what should be going in-and-out on a single day.*

Hamas and Al Fatah formed a Palestinian Unity government following their reconciliation talks in 2014 within the Gaza and the West Bank. The first coalition government was led by Rami Hamdallah. However it was anything but clear-sailing. The territory was blockaded by Israel and Egypt following an incident between Israel and the Hamas in 2014. Israel says the blockade is necessary to impede Hamas from rearming and to impede Palestinian rocket attacks. Egypt says it wants to prevent Gaza residents from entering Egypt. This has led to drastic reductions in daily necessities including medical supplies and food for the Gaza residents since 2008. A leaked UN report in 2009 warned that the blockade was *devastating livelihoods "and causing gradual "de-development* (Sara Roy*)*. It pointed out that glass was prohibited under the blockade. Gaza is viewed by some critics as an *open-air prison.*

Palestinian-Israeli problem

Palestinians and Jews had lived side-by-side for generations, sometimes in serious conflict and at other times in relative peace. As time passed there came to be a sort of truce between the two. Then World War II happened. Everything changed and in many cases for the worse. This ensuing Palestinian-Israeli conflict was one of the worst things that happened.

Adolf Hitler condemned the Jews, the Gypsies, the Russians, the homosexuals and a whole host of others to his infamous, shockingly cruel concentration camps. Many died or were killed in these camps.

No one can forgive Hitler or his henchmen for this brutality. At the end of the war, USA and Europe did not know what to do with the Jews. They (USA and Europe) were not ready to settle them on their lands. So, an alternative was necessary. Harking back to the dispersal of the Tens Tribes of Israel around the world, USA and UK arbitrarily decided to displace the Palestinians and give their land to the European Holocaust Jews in 1948. So, they armed the Jews and dumped them onto the land of Palestine with the carte blanche to do as they wished there. So began the Israeli-Palestinian problem. There was a mass forced exodus of Palestinians from their homeland. This could so easily have been avoided with a little forethought and some compassion for all by Great Britain, USA and France. Had they divided Palestine equally between the European Jews and local Palestinians and armed both or neither, the unsavoury situation, the bombing and killing and the bad feelings generated could have been avoided. Jerusalem should have been equally accessible to the Christians, Muslims and Jews since it is of equal importance to all three religions. Instead Donald Trump 'gave' Jerusalem to the Jews – a place of worship for all which was never his to 'give.' This only exacerbated the situation. To add to this, he also informed the Jews that the Gaza Strip was theirs – again not his to arbitrarily distribute.

Donald Trump has exacerbated the situation there by a few moves that he has made. All this has now led the area to become an even more volatile and dangerous place. We will soon reap the whirlwind from those decisions.

Syria

> *By fairy hands their knell is rung;*
> *By forms unseen their dirge is sung;*
> *There Honour comes, a pilgrim grey,*
> *To bless the turf that wraps their clay;*
> *And Freedom shall awhile repair*
> *To dwell, a weeping hermit there!*
>
> *Ode* written in 1746 William Collins

Bashar Al Assad is the President of the country and leader of the Ba'athist party. Its official name in English is the Syrian Arab Republic. In Arabic it is called Al Jumhuriyah al Arabiyah or-Suriyah. In 2011 there were successful uprisings in Tunisia and Egypt. Syria at this time was also having internal problems.

The problem started on 29 June 2011 in the city of Deraa after some young teenage boys wrote anti-government slogans: *The government must go* on a wall. Some were arrested and others ran away. Some shots were fired. This turned into civil unrest and violence escalated. The civil war was at first between the Sunni majority and Assad's Shia Alawite sect. By June 2013, 90,000 people were dead. This jumped to 250,000 by August 2016. At this point others started to get involved. The war is now extremely intertwined, some unrelated to the main issue. Each of the players in this tragic war has their own interests and agendas. The populace suffers. The airstrikes at night only heighten the death toll and the rivalries. But as is usually the case, others got involved and the problem got magnified until now it has become a major issue.

The key players in this tragedy are:

The Assad Regime - Syrian President Bashar Al Assad and the ruling party; Assad is confident of his position especially with the backing of Russia and Iran. He aims to consolidate his position which is already strong by eliminating the pockets of resistance. To this end he has used chemical weapons to frighten through terror. In this way apparently, less lives would be lost.

Russia – For the Russian President Vladimir Putin, the Syrian struggle encapsulates the central theme of his presidency and his legacy. He would like to restore Russia as a great power. Helping Assad means extending Russian power in the region. But at the same time, he does not want to get into a head-on confrontation with the USA. Russia backs Syria.

United States – Trump is obsessed with defeating Isis. The US does not want Russian power and prestige to increase nor do they want a head-on collision with Russia. So, neutral territory is best for confrontations. USA is also desirous of containing Iran's influence in the Middle-East. It is also a way to reverse Obama's policy because at every point, where possible, Trump has undone what Obama did. US backs the rebels.

Iran. –This is a predominantly Shia Muslim country. Assad's regime is Shia Alawite. So that bond is there. Then Iran and Israel are never on the same wave-length but on opposing sides. One country's gain is always the other country's loss. Iran sees Syria as a buffer zone – neutral territory. Syria could also be the conduit to supply the Hezbollah and Iranian militias in the Golan Heights. Iran can pose a serious threat to Israel. Iran does not want any confrontation with the USA, as long as US airstrikes are directed at chemical facilities. Iran backs Syria.

Israel - Iran and Israel are never on the same wave-length but on opposing sides. One country's gain is always the other country's loss. Israel also sees Syria as a buffer zone – neutral territory. Syria could also be the conduit to supply the Hezbollah and Iranian militias in the Golan Heights and so Israel would disrupt that. Israel backs the rebels.

Turkey: Recep Tayyip Erdogan was one of the most determined advocates for regime change in Damascus but is now seeking accommodation with the Syrian regime. This is because of Turkey's Kurdish problem. Erdogan hopes to break up the Kurdish hold of the territory along the Turkish-Syrian border. However, he has to be careful not to risk a confrontation with the Americans, who consider the Kurds as their most effective pawn against Isis. Turkey backs the rebel but would like an accommodation with Damascus.

United Kingdom: The UK sees its role as a partner in the anti-Isis coalition and, also its participation in strikes as an international non-proliferation responsibility, because it too is a permanent member of the UN Security Council. Britain is aware that the refusal to take part in planned punitive strikes in 2013 after an earlier chemical weapons attack has already weakened its relationship with Washington. So, it would redress that. UK goes where US leads. UK backs the rebels – the more moderate ones.

France: Emmanuel Macron has taken a particularly strong line on the use of chemical weapons, and like the UK, it sees participation in such strikes as necessary to retain status as a major power, by policing non-proliferation norms. Paris also sees the anti-Isis fight as being a national security imperative, given that it has been one of Isis's principal targets. France backs the moderate rebels.

Saudi Arabia: It has long tried to break the alliance between Iran and Syria. It also wants to dominate the Persian Gulf and the Middle East. Even more important it wants to stop any kind of unrest coming into Saudi Arabia. Also, there is its desire to have a regime in Syria more to its taste. It too, like the USA, supports the rebels.

UN Security Council Resolutions: Over 20 resolutions were passed until now to stop the fighting but the war is still going on. I believe because the big powers are involved and they do not really want to see an end to the fighting until they have succeeded in toppling Bashar al Assad and his regime. Nadin says and I agree with him that whenever the Security Council members are divided, nothing comes of the resolutions it passes.

According to the Lowy Institute paper:

The UN Security Council has unequivocally failed the Syrian people: over 400,000 of whom have been killed, over 5 million of whom are refugees, and around 6.3 million of whom are internally displaced.

The recent resignation of Carla del Ponte from the UN Commission of Inquiry on Syria is just the latest in a long line of UN officials who have quit their positions out of frustration with the lack of meaningful progress, on either peace or justice. Del Ponte, however, has directly singled out the culprit: the UN Security Council.

She said that she had expected *'to persuade the Security Council to do something for justice'. But, in the seven years of the Commission, 'nothing happened...we are going nowhere'.*

Justice, it seems will not be served in the short or long term. The Syrian case has not yet been opened. Interference by world powers in Syrian affairs can only have a negative effect as happened in other countries that world power (s) interfered with. Syrian internal affairs were for Syria and Syria alone to solve. Now it is a free-for-all there.

The UN, like the League of Nations earlier has failed the world because it has been hijacked by some powers. It has no voice of its own any longer. It cannot and does not protect the weak(er) from the super powers but plays into their hands. Meanwhile people – mainly civilians keep on dying. Countries keep on spiralling downwards into ruin and carnage. And the same ones who began the process of destruction see nothing, hear nothing and do nothing to stop this carnage.

The UN Security Council also failed to prevent and to respond to the situation on the ground in Syria. Article 2(7) that forbids interference in the affairs of an independent nation was not invoked. The question is why?

Major protests began in mid-March, and violence on a major scale was in full force due to too many parties involvement and too many diverse agendas had been initiated. And it is an accepted fact that once conflict begins, it is very hard to contain. The UN Under Secretary-General for Political Affairs B Lynn Pascoe briefed the Council at the end of April 2011 whereas the problem began much earlier and as we all know a problem can be resolved much more easily at its inception rather than when it is in full force.

According to Peter Nadin:

Kofi Annan's six-point plan; the deployment of the short-lived observer mission (United Nations Supervision Mission in Syria); the push for humanitarian access; and the establishment of the OPCW-UN Joint Mission in Syria were all well-meaning mechanisms. But the Council has remained largely on the sidelines, adopting only a handful of resolutions, many of which remain dead-letters (the Council was not even responsible for the creation of the mission of the UN Special Envoy to Syria – a post filled by Annan, Lakhdar Brahimi, and currently occupied by Staffan de Mistura).

Yes, vetoes were initiated but failed. Of the eight vetoes, six were deadlocked. The major powers each had their own axe to grind and so could not agree. Meanwhile people kept on suffering and dying. Bombs kept falling and the fighting kept on.

The case of Syria highlights the limits of global governance mechanisms in the face of complex situations. It is still premature to give up on the UN Security Council but, if it is to remain relevant in the future, it must perform better. Let's hope Syria is its nadir. (Peter Nadin)

See yonder poor, o'er laboured wight
So abject, mean and vile
Who begs a brother of the earth
To give him leave to toil
And see his lordly fellow worm
The poor petition spurn
Unmindful that a weeping wife
And helpless offspring mourn
                          Man was made to Mourn by Robert Burns

Venezuela's official name is the República Bolivariana de Venezuela or in English the Bolivarian Republic of Venezuela. It is located on the northern coast of South America. It has a number of small islands and islets in the Caribbean Sea as part of Venezuela. The capital city is Caracas which is also the primary centre for industry, commerce, education and tourism. To the north it is bounded by the Atlantic Ocean and the Caribbean Sea; to the east by Guyana; to the south by Brazil and to the southwest and west by Colombia.

Its top imports are refined petroleum, corn, wheat, ethers and rice. The top export destinations of Venezuela are the United States, China, India, Singapore and Spain.

A brief recent History

When in 1999 Hugo Chavez was elected as President, he found a country in dire straits greatly due to the privatizations that the IMF (International Monetary fund) imposed on Venezuela. There were days without electricity, garbage would not be collected and so on. Chavez restructured the government advocating a path between socialism and capitalism. He determined that profits from oil should go to the state and not to Wall Street corporations. This helped

Chavez in his goal of social programmes for the country. He was also the leader of the United Socialist Party of Venezuela (PSUV).

In 2002 there was an attempted coup against him which failed. After this Chavez announced that Venezuela would move towards a "21st Century Socialism". The very word Socialism makes the Capitalistic societies very uncomfortable. Countries with Socialism have done and are doing well, in spite of what the US says. Chavez also quoted Marx and Lenin in his TV addresses. He wanted to bring Venezuela forward by having a prosperous non-capitalist society. And he succeeded. Poverty and unemployment were cut by half by 2009. Literacy was on the rise. After Chavez died, Nicolas Maduro (Also of the PSUV) continued his policies. By the end of 2015 over one million modern flats had been constructed.

Problems that Venezuela now faces began in 2014 with oil. Venezuela is an oil based economy. In 2014 Saudi Arabia started spooking the market by supplying cheap oil. And this combined with the results of fracking had a very bad effect on the Venezuelan economy, but good for the US economy.

Present day

The US administration as is usual, being 'democratically inclined,' is creating another crisis. This time in Venezuela just as they earlier created for El Salvador and Honduras among other Central and South American countries. The result of US kindness to those countries has destroyed their way of life and now they are trying to go to the US for economic relief. US is unwilling to give them sanctuary. It was for that reason that many infants and children were separated from their parents on democratic US soil and put in cages. It was the decision of President Trump and his policy makers. Of course, it led to a public outcry from the US citizens.

This is not to forget US interference in other countries like The Former Republic of Yugoslavia where too, they wanted to establish 'democracy' by inciting rebellion. Now the FRY is broken up into smaller countries and all have a much worse standard of living. The same goes for Iraq and Libya where too, they wanted to depose an 'autocratic dictator' by murdering him and **imposing their brand of democracy.** All these countries used to be well off and enjoyed a very good social welfare status. Now they are poor and trouble within their boundaries will not stop. The latest lucky recipient is Venezuela.

The US has decided that Juan Guiado will be the president and Nicolas Maduro must go. But Venezuelans won't play ball. So, their trading ability is under attack and sanctions are imposed on them as is always the case when US decides on a preferred course of action.

Whenever the US wants to get rid of the leader of a country, it always brings out the card of dictator or Communist. US National Security advisor John Bolton as is his usual wont, has been pushing for war on Venezuela ever since the US recognised Guiado as the self-declared, not democratically chosen, interim president of the country at the end of January. He (John Bolton) is the same war hawk who successfully duped the Americans about Saddam Hussein's mythical horde of mass destruction weapons. That led to one of the worst, most catastrophic and despicable conflicts in modern history. It is still going on. There is no peace or safety there as will be the same in Venezuela if Bolton and others of the ilk succeed.

Elliot Abrams the master mind of the horrific killings in El Salvador and for the Iran-Contra scandal is pushing for Bolton to go as special envoy to Venezuela. It can only lead to political and social disaster and the poorest and most innocent will pay – as usual - for the decisions of people like Abrams and Bolton. Instead of further destabilising the situation in Venezuela, the US should be looking for a peaceful solution as Uruguay and Mexico are suggesting. Or the USA could just keep out of the affairs of Venezuela and leave them to solve their problems.

In the American mind, Communism and Socialism are equated with failure. This could be due to the long years of Cold War when we were all brainwashed with those ideas. In reality, however, Socialism and Communism at their best can and have done a lot for the countries that practised it. Today we hear that all Venezuela's troubles – the rioting in the streets, the empty shelves in the stores, the food lines, the inflation are all due to the dictator Maduro and Socialism. In truth it is due to the sanctions imposed on Venezuela, the cheaper and cheaper oil that Saudi Arabia, America's sidekick, is producing that is forcing the Venezuelan prices to spiral downwards and the political unrest in the country. Venezuela not in the distant past but in the recent past enjoyed the benefits of a Bolivarian type of economy. No one can be more of an autocrat with dictatorial powers than the Saudi Crown Prince. But of course, that is fine so long as Saudi Arabia toes the US line and does not dare step out of line. So Saudi produces cheap oil on demand by the USA to force down the prices of other oil-producing countries many of whom have US sanctions imposed on them like Venezuela.

The Venezuelan crisis is still to be resolved. If Madura loses, the condition of the area is going to deteriorate even further.

Yemen

Thomas Gray – *The Bard*

Yemen is the second largest independent Arab State and lies at the Southern end of the Arabian peninsula. It is also the poorest Gulf state country so you may wonder why Saudi Arabia, the richest Middle Eastern country is fighting there. It is certainly not to help Yemen. But Yemen is strategically a very important country as it sits on the strait connecting the Red Sea and the Gulf of Aden. Yemen sees a lot of the world's oil pass through this strait.

Yemen shares a border with Oman and the Arabian Sea in the East into which the Gulf of Aden flows, the largest border with Saudi Arabia to the North and is flanked by the Red sea to the West and the Gulf of Aden to the South.

The war here is complicated by many different players with different agendas like in Syria. (I think this is the way all future wars on foreign soil are going to be played out). There is Saudi Arabia who wants regional dominance while at the same time they would curb the power of the Shia Syrians. They (Saudi Arabia) tried to force the Prime Minister of Lebanon to resign in order to destabilize Lebanon and the region. **Saudi Arabia** is a Wahabi Sunni country and supposedly the protector of Islam. Fighting alongside the Saudis is the **USA** for reasons best known to themselves, besides their antagonism to the Syrian regime of Bashar al Assad. Also fighting shoulder to shoulder with Saudi Arabia is **Israel**. Israel is fighting here against the Hezbollahs who are also Shia Muslims but are a powerful bloc and control a large fighting force in Lebanon. In Yemen they are fighting the Houthis– a Shia sect as are the Yemenites since 2004. Poor Yemen is getting the worst of it. The country is destroyed and the people are in dire straits. Already millions have been displaced. But who cares!! Certainly not Saudi Arabia, the Protector of Islam! Children are starving. Children do not have medication. Children are dying every day. The children are innocent. We are looking at the deaths of innocents for no sin of their own or their parents but for lust for power among stronger nations.

The initial reason for this war lay in the failure of a political transition in 2011 that was expected to bring about peace by forcing the then president Ali Abdullah-Saleh to hand over power to Abdrabbuh-Mansour Hadi. That was the crux of the problem. Hadi failed to control the different groups. He was not and is not a popular person for president. There was the Jihadists, a separatist group in the south of the country; then there was the problem of a lot of security personnel who stayed loyal to Saleh and then there were the problems of unemployment, food shortages and corruption.

Earlier at the beginning of the century a minority of Zaidi Shia Muslims – the Houthi rebelled. They now joined forces with Saleh's supporters – the security forces loyal to Saleh against Hadi and soon they captured Saada Province in the northern heartland and the neighbouring areas. Meanwhile many ordinary Yeminites, disillusioned with Hadi, also joined the Houthis in late 2014. In 2015 they took Sanaa, the second largest city. They – the Houthis and loyal security forces and the disillusioned country folk then decided to take control of the whole country. Hadi fled abroad in March 2015.

In my opinion, Saleh should never have been forced to resign and hand over power to Hadi. All this would then have been avoided. I believe – I don't know – that other powers were behind that move to remove Saleh.

The Saudis were alarmed at the rise of this power. They believed that the Houthis were supported by Shia Iran and they cobbled together eight other, mostly Sunni Gulf states – Kuwait, Qatar, Bahrain, the United Arab Emirates and Oman alongside the USA (but of course – Saudia and USA are bosom buddies!!) and Israel joined in for the fun. Then began air strikes against Yemen in an attempt to restore Hadi's government. At this stage the coalition (the GCC or Gulf Cooperation Council along with Saudi Arabia) received logistical support from the US, UK and France. It became a free-for-all. The battle the Saudis coalition believed would last a few weeks at most is now in its fifth year. There does not seem to be an end to this pointless war.

In 2015 the coalition fearing what would happen next landed their troops in the southern port city of Aden. I believe that the US felt the same way as Saudi about Iran and suspecting Iranian help to the Houthis decided to physically enter the war. Moreover, US had to enter the war. It would irk them to sit on the sidelines.

In a few months the Saudi coalition and the Western coalition together managed to push out the Houthi coalition and re-establish the Hadi government. But there was already severe lack of basic services. Hadi remained abroad.

In the meantime, the Houthis who were still in Sanaa, maintained their siege of Taiz, the third largest city, and fired missiles from there into Saudi Arabia.

At this time fighters from the Al Qaeda Arabian Peninsula (AQAP) and their local rival group – the Islamic State Group (IS) took advantage of the chaos and seized territory in the south and carried out attacks especially in Aden.

In November 2017 when they fired a ballistic missile towards Riyad, Saudi Arabia responded by tightening its blockade on Yemen. It gave them the excuse of wanting to stop arms smuggling to the rebels by Iran. Iran denied these allegations. Food prices shot up. More in Yemen went hungry. More children died or sickened because of malnutrition.

In June 2018 The Saudi group launched an all-out attack on the sea port – the lifeline of three quarters of the country on Hodediah, the seaport, held by the Houthi rebels to break the stalemate. UN warned against it but the warring continued and months later both parties met in Sweden to discuss avoiding an all-out war in Hodediah. In December they agreed on a ceasefire until mid-January.

UN believes this is the worst man-made famine in history as Yemen slips inexorably towards the worst famine in a 100 years.

The UN also says that more than 6800 civilians have been killed and over 10,700 injured in the fighting since March 2015. Over half of the causalties are the result of the Saudi led attacks. But a US group puts the estimate at 60,000 civilians and armed men since 2016. This number is based on the reports of the incidents. Not all incidents are reported.

Thousands have also died of preventable causes – disease and malnutrition. Two-thirds suffer from food shortages. About two million children suffer from malnutrition and so are very vulnerable to disease. Basic health care is lacking. The largest cholera outbreak has affected about 1.2 million people and about 2,500 related deaths have been reported since April 2017. **More than 2.3 million people are still displaced.**

The alliance between the Houthis and Saleh's supporters collapsed in November 2017 for control of Sanaa's largest mosque. This was soon followed by the in-fighting in the pro-government group.

A UN report in 2018 says that about 100 civilians are killed or injured daily. UNHCR said last year 5,000 civilians were either killed or wounded. A fifth of the casualties were children. Most of the causalities were in the west and a large portion in the war-torn city of Hodediah. The greatest number of civilians who died were killed inside their homes (many while travelling or working on farms, markets, at their business sites or in other civilian areas.

Recently UNICEF released a document reporting that about **one child dies or is killed every 10 minutes.** The news was only picked up by Al-Jazeera and DW. It did not make headlines or even news elsewhere. In the same report the organization estimated that more than 400,000 Yemini children are at risk from starvation and about 2.2 million more need urgent medical care.

This is shocking and a crying shame to all the rich and powerful countries like Saudi Arabia, the Gulf States, US, UK, France to allow such a situation to continue. The children are innocent of any crimes yet they are paying the highest price while the aggressors sit in their comfortable offices and homes and order the death of children.

Since the beginning of the war more than 100,000 innocent people have been killed and 69 percent of the country is in need of humanitarian intervention. Three million people have been forced to flee.

Shame on all of us for allowing such a state of affairs to continue!

US Military bases around the world

The US has a stunning number of bases around the world. Many of the earlier ones no longer function but the number they still have is very impressive. I cannot and will not go into any details but simply name some of the countries where the bases do exist and are still very much functioning. In some countries there are only a couple or so but in some countries there are quite a few. I believe this number is dependent on the location of the country and its relationship to the USA.

AFGHANISTAN –	KYRGYZSTAN
BAHRAIN –	NETHERLANDS
BULGARIA –	PORTUGAL
CUBA	PUERTO RICO
GERMANY	QATAR
GREECE	RHODE ISLAND
GREENLAND	SAUDI ARABIA I
GUAM	SINGAPORE
ITALY	SOUTH KOREA
JAPAN	TURKEY
KOSOVO	UNITED KINGDOM
KUWAIT	

This is not a complete list.

From this list I get two things. The first is that the US has bases in almost all countries where it had problems or those countries that were with the Axis powers with the exception of the UK. And the second thing that I noticed is that all these are in working condition.

The Plight of Immigrant children at the Border

The moving finger writes; And having
writ,
Moves on: Nor all thy Piety nor wit
Shall lure it back to cancel half a line
Nor all thy tears wash out a word of it
Rubaiyat of Omar Khayyam By Edward Fitzgerald

The <u>Monroe Doctrine</u> of December 2, 1823 is the cornerstone of US foreign Policy. It is to this policy that the present Immigration problem at the border can be attributed. There were four main points of the policy that relates to the present immigration problem. They are

1. The United States would not interfere in the internal affairs of or the wars between European powers; (European policy towards their colonies was changing and many countries in the Americas were getting their independence)
2. The United States recognized and would not interfere with existing colonies and dependencies in the Western Hemisphere; (US planned to be a world power and would not tolerate any competing power within its sphere)
3. The Western Hemisphere was closed to future colonization; (America wished to be in total control of the Americas)
4. Any attempt by a European power to oppress or control any nation in the Western Hemisphere would be viewed as a hostile act against the United States (only the US intended to have that power).

In order to understand the present immigration debacle one must know at least a bit of the relevant history.

In 1904 Theodore Roosevelt declared the USA'S right to exercise "international police powers" through central and Latin America that were not European colonies. And it did so, brutally leaving behind deep scars till today. This history of intervention is inextricable from the contemporary Central American crisis of internal and international displacement and migration.

When the Europeans left, USA stepped into the vacuum. It exerted all sorts of control – economic and political especially. US imports filled their markets which meant their produce had problems fighting for the market space.

In the political sphere it was much worse. USA interfered in the affairs of all its neighbours. It destabilised countries. It promoted opposition parties and supported dictators and drug cartels. CIA was very busy. As these countries of Central and Latin America became unstable they came to the USA as immigrants. This is what led to the present immigration situation.

If you are a super power you try to make sure those around you are on your wave length or at least well-disposed towards you. (It is always better to have friends or at least not enemies around you). For example as Richard E. Feinbergs puts it so well *China is engaged in a high-profile charm offensive to overcome long-standing animosities and draw its Southeast Asian neighbors into its orbit, through trade agreements and massive infrastructure projects. The Russia of Vladimir Putin is working hard to regain influence in territories of the former Soviet Union, throughout Europe and Central Asia.* But Trump disagrees. His vision excludes all except his core voters. He wishes to make "America Great Again" by excluding all who disagree with him and especially excluding immigrants mainly Blacks and non-Whites. Into this group comes all Central and Latin Americans.

The question arises why so many Central and Latin Americans wish to seek asylum in the USA. The answer as I mentioned earlier, lies in the American interference and deliberate sabotaging of their democratically elected governments in favour of dictatorial ones who are more often than not, supported by the USA. Trump does not seem to realise that if you would be great, you need friendly not hostile neighbours; you need to calm down, not ruffle feathers around you; you need to cajole not threaten your friends and nearest neighbours.

This brings me to the main issue here: the terrible state of undocumented immigrants and more specifically the young children in the Border holding places.

After becoming president, in 2018, Trump announced his ***zero tolerance policy*** on unauthorized entry into the USA. This was followed by his signed executive order to keep these immigrants at the border together. But the problem here is: why then are 2,300 children already separated from their families and living under very inhumane conditions in border patrol holdings? Trump had promised to keep families together for as he had said it would not be a problem for his administration in maintaining *strong – very strong - borders*. But that is not the reality at the border. Families have been separated! Young children and even infants are on their own!

Politically and economically a lot of these Latin American and Central American countries are in dire straits. About a century of US meddling and interventions - military coups and plundering have undermined these countries. There is no longer democracy in those countries. Democracy is not allowed to flourish or even exist for then they could become economically independent and therefore politically viable. There now is poverty, there is instability and drug cartels rampant in these places – the places from where the bulk of immigrants come to the US for a better life for themselves but more specifically for their children. What irony!

On August 5, 2004 CAFTA (Central America Free Trade Agreement – Costa Rica, El Salvador, Guatemala, Honduras, Dominican Republic and Nicaragua) was the free trade agreement between the US on the one hand and the Central American and Dominican countries. It was the first such agreement between the US and the smaller developing countries. This deal benefited US exporters of petroleum products, plastics, paper, textiles, manufacturers of motor vehicles, machinery, medical equipment, electric and electronic goods, cotton and cotton products, wheat, corn and rice. There are no tariffs on most of these products and by 2025 there will be no tariffs on any of these products. The deal favours the US Not the CAFTA countries.

Besides the above it also improves customs administration and removes technical barriers to trade. It addresses government procurement, investment, telecommunications, electronic commerce, intellectual property rights, transparency, labor, and environmental protection. The member countries are

- The USA and on the other hand
- El Salvador: March 1, 2006.
- Nicaragua and Honduras: April 1, 2006.
- Guatemala: July 1, 2006.
- Dominican Republic: March 1, 2007.
- Costa Rica: January 1, 2009.

Economically the Central American and Dominican countries were lost. Their local products could not compete with the US goods.

For decades now, the US has been carrying out military intervention in these countries. It has consistently undermined democratic governments in these countries, carried out military interventions, which caused serious instability in the region which created a vacuum in which drug cartels flourished.

This above information clearly shows that the CAFTA countries are in a bad way – politically and economically. So they come to the USA for a better life.

Mark Putterman puts it very succinctly:

U.S. empire thrives on amnesia. The Trump administration cannot remember what it said last week, let alone the actions of presidential administrations long gone that sowed the seeds of today's immigration crisis. There can be no common-sense immigration "debate" that conveniently ignores the history of U.S. intervention in Central America. Insisting on American values of inclusion and integration only bolsters the very myth of American exceptionalism, a narrative that has erased this nation's imperial pursuits for over a century.

The Washington Post made a rare visit inside the facility (June 2019), *where adults and their toddler children were packed into concrete holding cells, many of them sleeping head-to-foot on the floor and along the wall-length benches, as they awaited processing at a sparsely staffed circle of computers known as "the bubble." Hallways and offices previously designated for photocopying and other tasks now held crates and boxes of bread, juice, animal crackers, baby formula and diapers.*

Border Patrol officials in Texas said that they were often forced to hold unaccompanied children for five to 15 days. Attorneys for children held in custody say such extended detentions are *a flagrant violation of the law, a 1997 consent decree known as the Flores Settlement Agreement, and CBP guidelines.*

Children should not be held in captivity under such conditions. Children should not be held in any sort of captivity! It affects them psychologically and physically and sometimes they never recover. The Washington Post reported that many had chickenpox and scabies, lice, the flu, and general malnutrition were also reported by reporters who had been there. Six children five from Gautemala and one from El Salvadore died while in Border Patrol custody. Another teenager died of the flu. A father with his two year old strapped to his body died while crossing the Rio Grande. Who knows how many more died. This is a sorry indictment on a rich, prosperous, first-world country!

Interference from others each with their own agenda for interfering leads to severe worsening of the situation. It is the same as in a relationship only much worse. If countries undergoing upheaval are left to sort out their issues, the problems are solved much more easily and with much less loss of life and property

To conclude, again as Putterman says: *It's time to insist that accepting Central American refugees is not just a matter of morality or American benevolence. Indeed, it might be better described as a matter of reparations.*

Trump – an Introduction

Donald J Trump, the 45th president of America has brought hate and divisiveness to the American scene by stoking these negative emotions. He has kindled the fires of hate, racism, xenophobia, and so on but denies all culpability. Being the president of USA, his behaviour is emulated by many. He is a racist as his own words his have proven over and over again. So, many people believe it is good to be a racist. After all they are only emulating the President!

Trump, like the infamous Senator Joseph McCarthy and Adolf Hitler is an opportunist and a demagogue. Combine the two and you have a dangerous mix. All three searched for an issue to base their demagoguery on. Hitler chose the Jewish problem as he saw it; McCarthy chose the Communist and Trump chose Making White America Great Again among other slogans that he had tried earlier. Both Hitler and McCarthy overreached themselves and brought about their own downfall. It was their hubris.

Trump is ideologically flexible and an opportunist. When he ran for the presidential election in 1987/1988, it was the Japanese he chose to discriminate against. This was because the Japanese economy appeared to be outstripping the American one which was making a lot of people nervous. So, he declared that the Japanese have *long faces* during negotiations and laugh behind the backs of the Americans at them. He did not go so far as to say that he witnessed it but that he strongly believed this to be the case. In 2000 when he again thought of running for the presidential elections he attacked Senator Pat Buchanan as being anti-Black. Lies came and come, even more so now, very easily to Trump as they did to McCarthy. McCarthy saw a Communist in every nook and corner and destroyed many, many lives. Trump is very anti-Black and against all non-whites. He has insulted American–Africans and people of Colour many times. He has called African countries *shit-hole* countries. He had asked that a 'C' be put on forms if a Black family wanted to rent any of his apartments. They were then rejected or given harsher conditions. But his bias does not stop here. He is also very strongly anti-Muslims. A few examples of this would his cutting off of all financial help to the Palestinians, his giving away of Jerusalem to Israel – Jerusalem is not his to give away. It is the heart of **three** religions – Christians, Muslims and Jews. This move of his has exacerbated tensions there. He has revoked entry for Muslims to the US. The list is long. Trump is also very anti-Gays and Lesbians and anti-abortion.

Trump gauged the situation well and decided to use his anti-Black bias in his latest presidential election bid (2016). He realised this during Obama's tenure as president. Trump made many false allegations against Obama going as far as to say he should not be the president as he was not born in the US but in Kenya. He also said Obama was a poor student. All these were asserted by Trump without any proof of any kind. Trump lied loudly and repeatedly about this. Many Republicans believed him, and still appear to do so even though he has been proven wrong and a liar.

In modern times he has created more ill will among Americans than any other president in American history. I really feel sorry for the great country America was, the beacon of hope it had stood for, until Donald J Trump!

The next point of attack for him was the targeting of skilled workers. Spouses (and children) – graduates who were legally allowed to work in the States (H--1B visas; since 2015) can no longer do so. His xenophobia stretches from building the wall along the Mexican border to the Muslim ban, to denying of work opportunities to foreign spouses of US citizens waiting for their US citizenship status. This *"Buy American and Hire American"* order was signed on April 18, 2017 by Trump which is based on the false dichotomy of pitting one group against another. Both lose in the process as there is a lot to be said of positive competition and no good to be said of xenophobic attitudes. Trump has directly contributed to the psychosis of white superiority and that Blacks and Coloured people are responsible for the downward spiraling economic crisis that has shifted the US economy from industrial to knowledge–based and added prohibitive costs for higher education to that.

On April 18, 2017, Trump signed the *"Buy American and Hire American"* executive order. The order sought to spur a rise in wages for American workers and stricter immigration standards for foreign workers. Trump's *"Buy American and Hire American"* is built upon the false dichotomy that pits American versus foreign workers, playing off the inescapable psychosis in white, working class communities across the United States that immigrants of Colour were the direct cause of their dire, and spiraling, economic condition. More universal societal ethos than hillbilly elegy, blaming black, brown and Asian foreigners was far more compelling an excuse for diminished employment prospects and rising debt, than the reality of the shift of the American economy from industrial to knowledge-based, and the prohibitive costs of higher education, as mentioned earlier.

Trump is a xenophobic and a racist and openly espouses these ideas. He is very often untruthful and so truth has become a victim. He lies so much and so often that it is impossible for anyone to keep track and to write them all down. Some brief examples would be: his attacks on Obama, his country of birth and education; his lying that four previous presidents supported his closing down of the Federal Government for 38 days; he also said that many who were directly affected by this, supported the move to close down the government – that was all untrue;…

His xenophobia and racism spills into many other aspects of his political life:

- Rejecting of globalism – his stigmatising of engagement and collaboration among nations, his association (misunderstanding??) of globalisation with the negative aspect only of ideology
- His advocating of economic nationalism
- His populism
- His racism and racist policies
- His insular attitude
- His breaking of deals because he didn't want to associate too closely with old
  friends like the UK, France, Germany, EU, South Korea among others.

Then there are his misogynistic and homophobic attitudes. There are too many times that he has shown openly and proudly what he thinks about others. For example: on winning the 2016 elections, one of the first things he did was to reinstate the *Global Gag Order* or the *Mexico City Policy* as it is also called. This was enacted by President Ronald Reagan but was rescinded by President Obama. According to this policy international organisations that receive help from the USA **cannot** offer services or information concerning abortion or any other service to women even if it is with their own money. This is harking back to the times when women did not have a voice in such personal matters. It is a bad policy because it severely restricts access to healthcare for women in need, resulting in increased rates of unintended pregnancy, pregnancy complications, and maternal mortality. It also does not help the victims in rape cases especially on campus rapes. Trumps administration has also rolled back the clock on women's rights to childbirth at home, taking birth control pills, evidence-based sex education etc.

It is not just in his policy that he is a misogynist but also in his tweets and speeches like when he sneered at this presidential opponent, Carly Fiorina looks by saying: *Look at that face! Would anyone vote for that?* Or even when he said about Hilary Clinton that she was a *nasty woman* and that if she couldn't *satisfy"* her husband, she *couldn't satisfy America.* His comments on women are generally cheap and vulgar.

There is also his homophobic attitude towards all non-whites but most especially against the blacks. Referring to them he had said in 1991 that *laziness was a trait in Blacks.* Another time he said: *Black guys counting my money! I hate it. The only kind of people I want counting my money are short guys that wear yarmulkes every day.* And he also said - contradicting himself as he often does: *I have a great relationship with the blacks. I've always had a great relationship with the blacks. Which statement are we to believe?* He also claimed *there were not enough jobs in America because Mexico and China had taken them.*

President Trump's political outlook has divided the USA and has led to the coming to power other similar nationalistic and extreme right-wing leaders in other countries. David Duke, the former leader of the Ku Klux Klan endorsed Trump and when he was asked about this he (Trump) was reluctant to disavow Duke or his support.

America was a beacon of hope, the land of the free, the land of liberty and opportunity. It should be so again!

Trump and Globalisation

Donald Trump often misuses and misunderstands words and terms. This leads to misunderstandings. It appears that to him globalisation is synonymous with ideology. The two are not the same. Ideology defines our individual values and beliefs; or in politics and economics, our system of ideas and their implementation. There are many ideologies and countries follow that which suits them best e.g. Communism is an ideology practised by China or Conservatism, practised by the party in power in Britain. Generally speaking there are five major ideologies: Anarchism, Absolutism, Liberalism, Conservatism, and Socialism (or Communism).

On the other hand, is Globalisation. In our fast shrinking world it is impossible to be anti-globalisation and still be a powerful partner. Globalisation is the process by which interaction and integration among people, companies, and governments and other institutions worldwide is carried out. It is a natural outcome of our technological advances in most spheres of our lives like transportation, communication, international trade, advances in medicine, science etc. It has grown in leaps and bounds due to these many factors. Globalisation is primarily an economic process of interaction and integration of social and cultural aspects. However, conflicts and diplomacy are also part of the historical development and the modernisation of globalisation.

In his 2018 United Nations address, Trump openly and unapologetically defended his adherence to anti-globalisation and for economic nationalism. He demanded US *independence and co-operation over global governance, control and domination.* During his speech he also embraced patriotism and rejected globalisation as the way of making America great again. This is a misconception on his part because he has mixed patriotism with nationalism. His desire to disconnect with the rest of the world and with America's close allies is dangerous. He has withdrawn from deals, turned away from friends, sowed divisions not only in his country among his people but also around the world. In many of his speeches he rants about how he will not allow the workers to be victimised but most of the victimisation comes from his divisive policies.

Historically, some elements in the American state and society, which were guided by Puritan values of responsibility and political correctness, under both Republicans and Democrats evolved to fit in with the changing times. However, since Trump took office, the American political system has been derailed by a *president who tends to ignore most American ideals and defies its institutions, by imposing his subjective claims, such as 'fake news', 'alternative facts', and his grandiose construct of 'principled realism'.* (Al Jazeera news). In front of the world leaders gathering in New York he said: *America's policy of principled realism means we will not be held hostage to old dogmas, discredited ideologies, and so-called experts who have been proven wrong over the years, time and time again.*

Trump has continually and consistently belittled diplomacy, international institutions and international pacts. His is an isolationist policy not only internationally but also internally (Cf. withdrawals), while the rest of the world works towards greater cooperation and globalisation. As a matter of fact, he has made several pledges for non-engaged, non-globalist, and non-committed America. He has pointed out his opposition to UNHRC by withdrawing from it by saying that the UNHCR is *a grave embarrassment to this institution [UN], shielding egregious human rights abusers while bashing America and its many friends.* He also viciously attacked the International Criminal Court (ICC), saying that it has *no jurisdiction, no legitimacy and no authority* and so he would never abide by any of its decisions. Populism, nativism, Islamophobia, Hispanophobia, anti-globalism, are his justification for extreme nationalism – not patriotism and this road can only lead to a White republic. Everything that a democracy must have, Trump rejects.

Trump, it appears, forgets that America is a part of the global world. And if America would continue to be a world leader, it has to be a part of the greater picture.

Trump and the EU

When in December 2015 Britain announced that it would withdraw from the EU, EU feared other countries would follow suit. But the opposite happened. The EU members rallied and support from member countries became stronger. Donald Trump's election in 2016 further strengthened the EU. The EU right-wing became stronger in their defense of the EU. One reason for this most probably is the fear of Trump's *"America First"* policy. Added to this is the idea of *us versus them* – and the EU thus views itself more as an unit that can depend on each other for protection from external threat – namely that from the USA. United they can even compete with the USA.

Trump's behaviour towards the EU instead of causing friction and division among EU members has in fact solidified them and resulted in progress in some areas like the Permanent Structures Cooperation (PESCO) in foreign and security policy. This was first initiated in 2017 and is a part of the EU security and defence policy.

EU's popularity has risen especially on the continent's mainland and many believe Trump becoming the US president could be the best thing for the EU. However, at the same time he poses a threat to world peace and harmony and a danger to igniting war with his withdrawal from various deals that were made towards establishing a secure world – (*Paris Agreement, Iran nuclear deal* etc.) and his overt threats to countries when things do not go his way. However, it must be pointed out that he narrowly averted war with Iran after the mining of the 2 ships and the shooting down of the drone. (Since then he has again changed his tune and is threatening war). Some members of his cabinet were quite soured by this, namely,

- John Bolton who has gone to Israel to underscore that war with Iran is very much a possibility
- Mike Pence who insists war is a serious probability and

- Mike Pompeo who has gone to Saudi Arabia and the Gulf States to shore up support against Iran and whisper war

War at the best of times is a bad decision. It is always much better to work out a deal. And Americans have no conception of modern war on their soil. The closest they have ever come was the American War of Independence and the American Civil war – neither of which had nuclear armaments or germ warfare. I must commend Trump's decision to desist from war in this instance. How far it will hold, none can say.

Trump is setting a new trend of ignoring or sabotaging political correctness and blatantly lying. But at the same time he does say out loud certain unpalatable truths that are usually swept under the rug.

Then there is the new breed of politicians who serve as both prime minister and interior minister like Hungary's Viktor Orban, Italy's Matteo Salvini and Trump's ever shrinking circle of ministers. This too is a dangerous trend because too much power is at the discretion of one person.

Perhaps as Max Hofmann, DW Brussels Bureau chief put so well is the lesson we should learn from the Trump presidency:

> *The EU is trying to use the momentum that the US president has brought to many issues of world and trade policy to its advantage. Trump has finally given the bloc the impetus to construct an EU that is not just important economically but has what European Commission President Jean-Claude Juncker called "Weltpolitikfähigkeit," which he defined as "the capacity to play our role in shaping global affairs."*

European Commission chief Jean-Clade Juncker is one of the few politicians who have taken Trump's measure. Though the US tariff of

25% on steel and 10% on aluminium remain for the time being they have agreed to avoid an all-out trade war. EU will buy more liquefied natural gas (LNG) and soybeans from the US. But their relationship stays very uneasy and fraught with suspicion.

Trump & Xenophobia

Xenophobia is the fear or hatred of what is perceived to be foreign or different. It involves perceptions of an in-group towards an-outgroup and manifests itself in suspicion of the outgroup's actions, motives etc. Alongside this is a desire to eliminate or remove their very presence in order to feel safe. Xenophobia is also a need to ensure racial or ethnic purity and/or national identity. Xenophobia is often confused with racism. Though they often go hand-in-hand, they are not quite the same. Xenophobia is prejudice and maybe hatred based on external appearances, nationality and culture. (We hate that which we fear – a truism). Whereas racism is based on fear, dislike or even hatred of a people's **racial** heritage.

In the recent past there has been a marked upsurge in xenophobia and racism especially in the US. In Donald Trump's speech in June 2015 referring to the immigrants from Central and South America, he said "*they are bringing drugs, bringing crime; they are rapists'* with absolute certainty. The stage was set for a rocky ride as Trump stirred the pot of xenophobia and racial tensions. He often uses the term *infect, infectious, vermin, rats* when referring to the immigrants and some areas in the States. This kind of language is offensive to all, inflammatory and derogative. America is the home of democracy of opportunities. It should stay that way. But as the election is getting nearer, Trump seems to be using inflammatory language more. Perhaps it is one of his 2020 campaign lines. And it should be remembered that 17% of the population are Hispanics. They took exception to Trump's statement. And after he won the election, it only got worse. His xenophobic vision of America is inciting racial violence. I agree with Mark Rubio when he says that Trump's comments are *offensive and inaccurate,...and divisive.*

According to Suman Raghunathan (January 27, 2018) attacks against Muslims, South Asians, Sikh, Hindu and Middle Eastern communities living in the US has risen by a staggering 45 % in 2017, since Trump became President. This is a very tragic state of affairs. After all even Trump's family as well as that of his three wives families are immigrants – two of the three being recent immigrants and one Marla - her family came to the USA in the mid 17th century.

As the world gets smaller and smaller due to globalisation, we should be able to accept others, not stand in judgement on them based on their country of origin. There are more and more mixed marriages around the world and here we have a president advocating regressing to much earlier times. Trump's policies have created a much less safe, pluralist and tolerant country. And sad to say a lot of Republicans echo him, though in a more subdued manner or by keeping silent. Silence is assent as any court of law will tell you. And when we are silent in the face of intolerance and hate, we are silent partners in it. Hitler's Germany is a case in point. Had there been strong dissenting voices, there would never have been the concentration camps or a holocaust that we all regret today.

Trump's Islamophobia is hard to understand as well as that of the GOP. In the aftermath of the Paris attack Islamophobia has taken a turn for the worse all over and the question of national identity has become an urgent and fast-spreading issue. Trump's racial policies are echoed by most of the GOP and they envisage a much less pluralistic and much more intolerant country – a country in which your religious adherence could easily lead to rejection, suspicion and worse much like in Hitler's Germany. Both Hilary Clinton and Bernie Sanders have argued against Trump's policies and advocated for a much more tolerant and pluralistic country, in this the 21st century as the world keeps shrinking due to our massive advancement in technology.

Before the last election, NBC interviewed Trump and one question was how such (racist and xenophobic society) a situation in America would be inherently different to that of Nazi Germany in the 1930's onwards towards the Jews. Trumps simply shrugged and curtly said *you tell me*. But the frightening truth is that we <u>are</u> going in that direction. USA leads the way and we follow.

In another interview with Hunter Walker of Yahoo, Trump acknowledged that he wanted a radical change in the treatment of American Muslims. Most of the Republicans in the Senate repeated, albeit in a weaker tone, what Trump said. The only dissenting voices were those of John Kasich and Jeb Bush.

A few Democrats – (47 to the Republican 242) also supported the anti-immigration and anti-refugee stance of the government. On the whole, the Democrats have criticised Trump for these policies. Bernie Sanders in a speech at the Georgetown University, in June 2015 said: *Donald Trump and others who refer to Latinos and peoples from Mexico as criminals and rapists, if they want to open that door, our job is to shut that door. This country has gone too far. Too many people have suffered and too many people have died for us to continue to hear racist words coming from major political leaders."* Hilary Clinton speaking to the Council on Foreign Relations (June 2015) said: *Turning away orphans, applying a religious test, discriminating against Muslims, slamming the door on every Syrian refugee, that is just not who we are,"* ... *"We are better than that."*

Trump, Sanders, and Clinton have one thing in common: They all recognize that aspirational ideals about what is America is the key to our politics. For Trump, American greatness comes from defeating foes, which might mean doing some previously "unthinkable" things to Muslim Americans. For Sanders and Clinton, America's greatness comes from its pluralism and rejection of bigotry. Which vision of America will win out is quite possibly the highest stake in the 2016 election (Jeet Heer). And as we now know – Trump's vision won.

Trump's xenophobia has led to the implementation of his racist policies. For example the removing and forcibly taking small and older children from their asylum-seeking parents and putting them in cages, is at the least, inhumane. We know about at least the death of one child while in a lockup. How many others were there? *Man's inhumanity to man/Makes countless thousands mourn* (Robert Burns – *Man was Made to Mourn*). What is there to say?!!

Trump and McCarthyism

McCarthyism

Communism has long been America's bugbear. As early as 1938, an organisation was set up called *The House of Un-American Activities Committee*. This committee was empowered by the authorities to investigate any movement or person(s) who apparently threatened the safety of the country. At this time Joseph Raymond McCarthy was a circuit judge.

World War II ended in 1945 leaving the world divided into two power blocs – USA and USSR, which hardened over the next 5-10 years. The US at this time became obsessed with what it perceived as the threat of Communism. It was also fast losing its monopoly as the only nuclear power after its nuclear threats against a number of countries and most specifically the USSR (See *Betrayal A political Documentary* by Ashley Smith chapter on USA pp 493-497). This lead to a nuclear weapons race and in September 1949 USSR exploded its first A-bomb. Meantime US had also got involved in fighting in Korea – again, because the US said it had to stop the tide of Communism spreading in Asia. Communism was spreading fast. Mainland China was securely Communist. Many in the US felt threatened that it might undermine and destroy their Capitalistic society.

In 1945 McCarthy was elected to the Milwaukee Senate. He achieved fame through his **unsubstantiated** accusation that 250 Communists had infiltrated the US State Department. Communist fear was at its peak in the USA. In 1953 he became the chairman of the powerful Permanent Subcommittee on investigations and began his terrible persecution of the American populace – like an inquisitor- -in his paranoid searching for Communist sympathisers among the Americans. And America is a free country! Perhaps McCarthy forgot that!

Any criticism of the government – no matter how constructive or innocuous became, to McCarthy, an admission of Communist sympathy or adherence to its values. Witnesses brought before the committee were **forced** to admit their guilt, but worse still, were also **forced to name and implicate others** – those they'd seen at meetings, held discussions with, known perhaps 10-20 years earlier. Liberal writers, filmmakers, actors – all – were forced to appear before the committee. Those actors, filmmakers who appeared before the committee were unable to find work later in any US film industry or theatre. His hectoring cross-examinations, his damaging innuendos, his arraigning of so many innocent civilians looked suspiciously like the Salem Witch-hunt of 1692 and somewhat similar (having much less power than Stalin) to Stalin's harassing of the Russians.

By 1956 his power was on the wane and finally he overreached himself when he clashed with the army. He was formally condemned by the US Senate and lost what remaining support that he had had among the Republicans.

This anti-Communist witch-hunt, often against the innocent, came to be known as McCarthyism.

USA has never really recovered from the fear of Communism. All its policies, with a few exceptions, since 1945, to a greater or lesser extent have been influenced by this fear.

Trump, like McCarthy can shift his ideological goal post and when in 1987 he went for the presidential election, he used Japan as his scapegoat because its economy was overtaking that of the US. It didn't matter what deals USA had with Japan. He suggested that the Japanese were not to be trusted because they never showed any emotion on their faces. So he suggested *Whatever Japan wants, do the opposite.* (at a rally in New Hampshire 1987).

In 2000 Trump again decided to enter the presidential election but now as a centrist. So he left the GOP for Ross Perot's Reform Party saying *the Republicans are just too crazy.* He went so far as to attack his opponent (Pat Buchanan) for being anti-Black.

Again, like McCarthy, he knows the power of fear and how to stoke it for his personal gain. So like McCarthy, he plays on the White Americans fear of the Blacks and people of colour. These are two very powerful weapons in his arsenal. He first realised this when Hilary Clinton said that Obama was not really American **in his thinking** and Obama's critics vociferously questioned his American-ness. It suited Trump to a 't' and with Roy Cohen's teaching to aid him he found his scapegoats – non-whites and Muslims. Early on Trump realized the power of fear. After all, he had for his teacher Roy Cohen his father's lawyer who also had coached Joseph McCarthy. Trump again looked around for a suitable scapegoat and found two to suit his purpose – race and religion.

McCarthy during the Red scare pulled out a paper and said he knew for certain 205 Americans in the government were Communist spies but he never showed the paper or the names to anyone. Similarly, in 2011 Trump saw his opening. *I have people that have been studying (Obama's birth certificate) and they cannot believe what they're finding. If he wasn't born in this country, which is a real possibility... then he has pulled one of the great cons in the history of politics. How does a bad student go to Columbia and then to Harvard? I'm thinking about it, I'm certainly looking into it. Let him show his records.* And yet Trump lies everyday and has been caught out and strangely enough he will not allow his University results to be released nor his tax returns! What a strange world! What goes around comes around!!

Both McCarthy and Trump are bullies. They manufacture evidence and browbeat their victims and scare their supporters. Both their parties (The Republican Party) cowered before them and rarely stood up to them. The Late John McCain won a lot of respect for standing up to Trump but even after McCain death, Trump attacked him and his daughter. McCarthy was more successful at it only because Trump does not have the same power in spite of being the President. There is also the political situation. Americans feared Communism enough to give credence to McCarthy's attacks. The Blacks and non-White people have a voice today. So Trump has constraints that McCarthy did not have.

Both are opportunists and grab or mould opportunity as the need arises. Neither pays much attention to the truth or the facts. Opportunity is their truth and their fact.

McCarthy especially disliked the Communists, Progressives, intelligentsia and Gays and did all he could to break them. One of the few people to go up against him at the height of his power was Margaret Chase Smith of Maine while delivering a speech called the "Declaration of Conscience" in 1950, Smith said in part, *"Those of us who shout the loudest about Americanism in making character assassinations are all too frequently those who, by our own words and acts, ignore some of the basic principles of Americanism—The right to criticize; the right to hold unpopular beliefs; the right to protest; the right of independent thought. The exercise of these rights should not cost one single American citizen his reputation or his right to a livelihood, nor should he be in danger of losing his reputation or livelihood merely because he happens to know someone who holds unpopular beliefs."*

Most people including the Kennedy family were afraid of McCarthy. The GOP dared not go against him and when a motion was brought against him, it was dismissed.

The GOP is wax in Trump's hand especially Mitch McConelly and Lindsey Graham. Only McCain had dared to call Trump to task. Mitt Romney said Trump's *endorsement is a delight*. He asked Trump to be his campaign surrogate in 2012. And when Trump during his presidential candidacy called Mexicans *rapists*, the Republican National Committee said he was a *high-calibre candidate*.

McCarthey lost his power by overreaching himself by attacking the US Military. It was the last straw. And in December 1954, USA heaved a sigh of relief as McCarthy's political career ended.

For Donald Trump, we have to wait and see.

Even while on the election campaign trail the seed of this attitude was present. When he said *Make America Great again*, he was in fact harking back to the time before the emancipation.

His lack of respect for the football players was clearly apparent when they took a leg during the anthem. Trump used very inappropriate language on them. Then he has consistently picked on Obama, going so far as to demand to see his birth certificate. He has called African countries S—thole countries and so on. The list is very long. There is also his attitude towards the asylum seekers from Central America and especially the Triangle. He has frightened his base into believing that they (Central Americans) are drug addicts and killers – even the little children.

Like McCarthy he is a demagogue and an opportunist. But where McCarthy theme was Communism, Trump's is people of colour, race and religion.

Trump and Racism

Trump has revived racism once more in The US which was underground for the past many years. Once again militant racism is on the move. This is not limited to one thing only but many. For example, there is the racial discrimination against the Blacks as was obvious in the verbal abuse Trump hurled at the NFL players for taking a leg during the National anthem. It could have been done much more subtly and decently without name-calling. Then there was the Charlottesville debacle when President Trump's core supporters brandishing anti-Jewish sentiments killed a young woman. All Trump had to say was that: *There were many good people on both sides...*

Trump's racism is bringing out the dormant racists that abound in his core group of followers as well as setting a trend not just in the US but also in Europe as is clearly visible by the many Rightist regimes now in power. The sad truth is, I believe, we are heading for a major catastrophe – perhaps even a world war.

There is a multitude of examples that show his crass racism and one could write a whole book on it. Suffice it to say that Trump is normalising racism and setting a bad precedent as he will be and already is being imitated as more and more are publically venting their hatred against other races, religions and colours. Roseanne Barr is a case in point with her racist utterances. She called Valerie Jarrett, an African American *an ape* and George Soros a Jewish Holocaust survivor *a Nazi collaborator* – among the myriad of other racist comments that she has made. She is much appreciated by President Trump as he has openly said time and again. She on her part feels emboldened to voice her racist views.

And not just Blacks and Hispanics, he has since a long time he has denigrated and attacked the Native Americans. There was the time when he was fighting competition for his Casino he had said: *Mohawk*

Indian record of criminal activity is well documented... This too was an untruth. The as recently as February 2019 in a tweet he mocked Senator Elizabeth Warren Native American heritage by poking fun at the Trail of Tears when the Native American were forced into an exodus from their land and thousands died on that trail. He is very critical of Latino s but he hired them for very poor pay to work in his homes and hotels.

Civilized society must give public affirmation to principles and standards, categorical norms, notions of right and wrong. Even though public figures often fall short of these standards...it is nevertheless crucial that we pay tribute to them. (Bill Bennet quoted in Max Boot's column May 30, 2018). This is a truism that all should follow for this is the sort of attitude that differentiates us from the war mongers and racists.

Trump's racism is not a new thing. As far back as 1973 he and his father were fined by the courts for housing discrimination at 39 sites around New York. *The government contended that Trump Management had refused to rent or negotiate rentals 'because of race and color', The New York Times* New York City 1975. Coloured people were offered different rental terms than those offered to the Whites. The Trumps then hired Roy Cohen, the lawyer of the infamous Joseph McCarthy. The Trumps finally settled the suit for $100 million and were to be reviewed regularly. Trump said this was *absolutely ridiculous*, (David Graham, January 2017), even though there are court documents to prove the truth of the charge. Then in 1989 he took out some ads in New York newspapers urging death penalty to be brought back for five Black and Latino teenage offenders. He seems to be negatively obsessed with dark skins.

Trump has termed the immigrants from Central America *animals* and said *they breed like animals. He also said that they were bringing diseases into the country.* He says (a lie) that mostly MS13 are coming in through the borders. Most asylum seekers coming to the States through the Mexican border are women and children and not MS13 people.

He insisted that President Obama was not born in the US and demanded to see his birth certificate (another lie) but he won't even show his tax returns. One wonders why – what could be so compromising that he won't allow the courts to see those papers?

His racism is not just against the Blacks and Coloured people. His supporters attacked the Jewish synagogue in Pittsburg. Eleven people died and four police were injured. This was one of the worst attacks against Jews in America in modern times. And it was in a synagogue. A few days later Trump announced that he was a Nationalist and shortly after this announcement 14 pipe bombs targeted the top Democrats.

Then there is his blanket ban on Muslims entering the US. He also said – totally without a shred of evidence – that when the World Trade centre came down he saw a film on TV that showed people cheering (Trump said they were Arabs). No one else saw that programme nor knew anything about it except Carson from Fox – Trump's blind supporter. It was another one of his lies.

When freedom of speech and action becomes untenable, it becomes dangerous. Leaders must be careful of what they say and do because their followers take from that what they think the leaders want them to and how they want them to act.

Trump is setting a very dangerous precedent which can easily get out-of-hand.

Economic Issues

Ring out the want, the care, the sin,
       The faithless coldness of the times;
Ring out, ring out my mournful rhymes,
But ring the fuller minstrel in.

Ring out false pride in place and blood,
       The civic slander and the spite;
       Ring in the love of truth and right,
Ring in the common love of good.

Ring out old shapes of foul disease;
       Ring out the narrowing lust for gold;
       Ring out the thousand wars of old,
Ring in the thousand years of peace.

Ring in the valiant man and free,
       The larger heart, the kindlier hand;
Ring out the darkness of the land,
Ring in the Christ that is to be.
       From *In Memoriam A.H.H.*
       Lord Alfred Tennyson

Deals – Some withdrawals and renegotiations

Since becoming President, Donald J Trump has withdrawn the US from many treaties and alliances. This makes for a more dangerous and polarised world.

Intermediate Range Nuclear Forces Treaty (INF)

This treaty was to eliminate nuclear missiles between USA and USSR. They could not agree on common ground and on each other's suggestions. Finally, in late 1977, NATO's Nuclear Planning Group presented a study showing that the Alliance's long-term INF modernisation needs in harmony with flexible response capability. The Special Consultative group was formed and in a document – the Decision Document – the principles and aims of the Alliance were set down

The U.S. approach to the negotiations, developed through extensive consultations within NATO, required that any INF agreement must:

1. provide for equality both in limits and rights between the United States and the Soviet Union;
2. be strictly bilateral and thus exclude British and French systems;
3. limit systems on a global basis;
4. not adversely affect NATOs conventional defense capability; and
5. be effectively verifiable

At first the USSR rejected it. The document was reworked on and by 1985 some progress had been made. USA and USSR agreed to have three different areas of partnership viz.:

- Nuclear and Space Talk (NST);
- Strategic arms and defence and space issues (START) and
- The Intermediate Range Nuclear Forces (INF).

Each side would have one delegate from each area. The deal was closed by the then Secretary of State George Shultz and the Soviet Foreign Minister Andrey Gromyko.

Finally, in February 1987 USSR said it was ready to reach a separate agreement with the USA. Then by the end of the year the treaty was signed by the then Presidents Ronald Reagan and Mikhail Gorbachev.

This led to the cold war when the world enjoyed a period of peace and relative quiet. There was a balance of power. The world sighed in relief!

Since Donald J Trump became the President of the USA, he has withdrawn from many treaties. The INF is one of those. On February 1, 2019 Trump announced his intentions. This would come into effect by Saturday February 5, 2019. On Saturday President Vladimir Putin announced that Russia too would no longer adhere to the terms of the treaty.

The problem now is: Are we going to begin with another faster and much more dangerous arms race? Or has it already begun only we are not aware of it. Only time will tell.

Trans-Pacific Partnership (TPP) – withdrawn 2017
It was a trade agreement between USA, Canada, China, Australia, Brunei, Chile, Japan, Mexico, Malaysia, New Zealand, Singapore, Vietnam and Peru. It was supposed to be ratified on February 4, 2016. It became defunct after the US withdrew its participation from the trade deal. One reason why Trump did so could be because it was one of his election promises. How far this is a clever move is hard to tell because as the US looks inward, the playing field would be left free for new alliances to be made and new trade deals will come into effect which will leave the US out in the cold.

<u>The United States Korean Free Trade Agreement_ renegotiated</u>
The agreement was signed on June 30, 2007 but came into full force on March 15, 2012. Until the US withdrawal and renegotiation of the deal, KORUS was America's sixth largest trading partner and seventh largest US export market. The reason for renegotiating the deal was that Trump felt it was unfair that the South Korea exported more to the US than the US did to South Korea. The new deal is basically the same with a few changes here and there.

US Ambassador Robert Lighthizer and Korean Minister for trade Hyun Chong Kim announced the renegotiated deal on March 28, 2018. This was one of the deals that the US renegotiated and did not summarily withdraw from. US has a military base in South Korea.

<u>NAFTA</u> established in January 1994 –Trump wishes to renegotiate but Congress must ratify.

NAFTA or the North American Free Trade Agreement was an agreement ratified by Canada, Mexico and the USA. It is the North American trade block. USA and Canada signed the bilateral deal on January 1, 1989. Mexico entered the deal in 1991 and it came into effect on January 1, 1994. According to this deal tariffs and duties were progressively eliminated on a wide range of goods except on a few agricultural produce. Trade, agriculture, textiles automobile manufacture were the main focus. The deal also sought to establish dispute resolution mechanisms, protection of intellectual property and implantation of environmental issues.

NAFTA (North American Free Trade Agreement) is a treaty among USA, Mexico and Canada. According to a journal from the Law and business Review of the Americas (LBRA) US public opinion shows that there are three things that NAFTA centres around:

- NAFTA's impact on the creation and destruction of American jobs

- NAFTA's impact on the environment and
- NAFTA's impact on immigrants entering the US

In a way NAFTA reshaped the economic relations among the three signatories but when Donald Trump became president, he decided to renegotiate the deal. While campaigning Trump had declared the NAFTA was *the worst deal* ever signed by the US. He believes that NAFTA impacts on the creation and destruction of American jobs. He withdrew from the deal but rethought and renegotiated it under the name United States-Mexico-Canada Trade Agreement (USAFTA) or United States-Mexico-Canada Agreement (USMCA) as it is also known as, to take effect from 2020 after the three countries separately ratify the deal.

G 7 June 10, 2018. The world reeled in shock at the oil crisis which led to a financial crisis. Heads of state of six countries decided to meet and come together to do something about their common problem. These were all industrial countries – France, UK, West Germany, USA, Japan and Italy. The idea was proposed by President Valery Giscard d'Estaing of France and Chancellor Helmut Schmidt of West Germany. They met at Rambouillet in 1975 to discuss the global economy and how to end the financial crisis and find ways out of the recession. **The Rambouillet Declaration** was signed and announced. In 1976 Canada joined and it came to be called the G7. In 1998 Russia joined and it became the G 8 but after Russia's annexation of Crimea it was excluded and the group went back to being called the G7. The member states France's President Emmanuel Macron, UK's Prime Minister Theresa May, West Germany's Chancellor Angela Merkel, USA's President Donald J Trump, Japan's Shinzo Abe, and Italy's Prime Minister Guiseppe Conte last met on June 8-9 2018 in Canada to discuss and find solutions, if possible, to topical issues like Climate change, commerce trade etc. President Trump did not agree with the economic section and withdrew from the G7 group in June 2018 amid acrimonious words and imposition of tariffs. USA also wants Russia reinstated in the G7 group.

<u>The UNHRC</u> was established to proclaim the rights of peoples of the world irrespective of race, colour, creed, religion or any other factor, in the United Nations General Assembly Resolution 217A on 10 December 1948. For the first time it set down fundamental rights to be protected universally. It has been translated into over 500 languages.

Washington: *The Trump administration has withdrawn from the United Nations Human Rights Council, making good on a pledge to leave a body it accused of hypocrisy and criticised as biased against Israel. For too long, the Human Rights Council has been a protector of human rights abusers, and a cesspool of political bias*, Nikki Haley, the US ambassador to the UN, said on Tuesday at the State Department in Washington (Nick Wadhams, June 20, 2018). This was not really a quick decision because the US has often criticised the UNHRC for bias against Israel for its human rights' abuses against the Palestinians and other minorities within Israel. Moreover, it has also been a forum for criticism of Trump's economic policies and the separation of children from their parents who are undocumented immigrants. Speaking to Al Jazeera from New York, Louis Charbonneau, the UN director at Human Rights Watch, said: *Unfortunately the US is placing protecting Israel from criticism for its abuses over all else* (Al Jazeera).

Philip Alston, the UN rapporteur, on poverty, in his report said President Trump's tax overhaul *overwhelmingly benefitted the wealthy and worsened inequality.* According to the report: *The policies pursued over the past year seem deliberately designed to remove basic protections from the poorest. It appears that under Trump the rich get richer and the poor, poorer.* Trump hates being criticised or admitting his mistakes. This must have galled him. It is no wonder that he withdrew from UNHRC.

US withdrew from the organisation in June 2018. This decision to withdraw from the UNHRC came after they launched a probe into recent killings in Gaza and accused Israel of using excessive force against the Palestinians of Gaza.

UNESCO The United Nations Educational, Scientific and Cultural Organization was established to promote peace and harmony between nations through amicable means. The constitution was signed and ratified on November 16, 1946. This is a specialised agency based in Paris. It has 193 members and 6 associate members. It helps in the building and rebuilding of their needs. Its goal is to alleviate poverty, disease, etc. and raise the standard of life in the developing world. It aims to harmonise educational opportunities between the genders. It is also still trying to implement national strategies in developing countries to have sustainable development. It is also responsible for heritage protected sites and environmental conservation.

US withdrew from UNESCO on December 31, 2018. US gave as its reason for withdrawing from the organisation

- that it was biased against Israel, US opposes any move by any UN body to recognise the Palestinian territories as a state;
- The US government's mounting arrears with them,
- and what US believes is UNESCO's need for reform. However, the US still wants to have a permanent observer status there.

The head of UNESCO, Irina Bokova, called the US withdrawal a *loss to multilateralism*, while UN Secretary General Antonio Guterres said through a spokesman that he *"regrets this development deeply.*

NATO or the North Atlantic Treaty Organisation was formed at the end of World War II which was so horrific that the world decided to join together and prevent any such horror from ever occurring again. The North Atlantic Treaty Organisation or NATO as it is more commonly known as, was established on April 4, 1949. The original members were 12 in number – Belgium, Canada, Denmark, France, Iceland, Luxembourg, the Netherlands, Norway, Portugal the

United Kingdom and the United States. In due course of time seven more countries were added. It stood at 29 countries – 27 in Europe including Turkey, and USA and Canada. Its purpose is to safeguard the freedom and security of all its members working together as one unit through *political and military means.* So, article 5 of the treaty clearly states that if a member state is attacked it will be deemed as an attack on all its member states. Cohesion, solidarity and collective defence, military or otherwise, is at the core of what NATO stands for. Besides this NATO is also the transatlantic link by which North American security and that of Europe is interdependent.

Relations between the US and NATO go up and down as US needs its support or not. When the US determined to bomb Yugoslavia, NATO was important in giving 'legitimacy' for the bombing and dismembering of Yugoslavia and the establishment of the largest US military base – Bondsteel under KFOR - in Europe based in the newly created state of Kosovo. Trump feels NATO is not useful in any way, relationship between the two have soured. On the campaign trail Trump referred to NATO as 'obsolete'. In fact there have been issues between NATO and its member states since 2000. US presidents since Clinton have not been as close to NATO as they once were. They have questioned if the "new" security challenges really fall under the aegis of NATO.

Trump decided to attend the NATO summit but he came an hour late and left early for his meeting with President Putin in Helsinki. It was an uncomfortable summit. Most of the leaders didn't know what hit them. No one was prepared for someone like Trump.

The last few US presidents and especially Trump insist that all allies must spend 2% of the country's GDP on the organisation. Some meet the goal (US, UK, Greece, Estonia and Poland) but many fall short. Also, NATO does not have a central role in the cyber and the 'grey-zone' warfare that is currently going on. And most shocking to NATO was Trump's announcement that the US would withdraw from the alliance. Later in 2017, Trump relented and said it would stay on condition all countries spent 2% of their GDP.

The Trump-NATO situation shows how worrying Trump's open suspicion of existing U.S. alliances and commitments has been on the world stage. The NATO summit was reportedly carefully tailored to him. The agenda was confined to counterterrorism and burden-sharing — two issues that are important to Trump. The problem of Russia was not on the agenda to cater to Trump. Also, members were asked to keep their remarks short, again to cater to Trump's attention span.

Trump's withdrawal of some forces from Afghanistan and Syria shocked his cabinet and led to the resignation of Jim Mattis, the then Defence Secretary. It also left Trump allies and officials at NATO headquarters nervous and nonplussed. Trump demanded that the members raise the 2% to 4 %. He also pointed out that most of the countries do not meet the 2% level. The member states did not agree. Trump threatened to withdraw from the alliance.

Withdrawal from NATO was in process but the US Congress House of Representatives - passed a bill in January 2019 that sought *to bar President Donald Trump from withdrawing from NATO.*

WTO OR World Trade Organisation : This is another intergovernmental organisation that regulates trade between nations. It was officially established in January 1, 1995 under the Marrakesh Agreement. It has 124 members. It replaced the GATT (General Agreement on Tariffs and Trade) agreement that had been in effect since 1948. It is the largest international body to date. It is located in Geneva, Switzerland.

WTO deals with trade regulation, services, intellectual properties ownership (TRIPS or Trade related Aspects of Intellectual Properties), especially among member states.

It has been successful in its mission and trade has flown much more smoothly in its presence than in its absence. For example, of the 26 cases the Obama administration filed in the DSB, mostly against China, US won most of them. But if Trump first imposes tariffs on others it would violate NAFTA and WTO rules. Those countries (China and Mexico) would retaliate and all would be dragged into a WTO dispute proceeding.

In August 2018, Trump informed Bloomberg News that if the WTO didn't "shape up", he would withdraw from it. However, his administrative body is not so keen to do so. Wilbur Ross, the Commerce Secretary, told CNBC in July 2018 that it was "premature" to discuss this. However, he said reforms to WTO were needed.

Trump and EU

Apparently, Trump dislikes the EU. He often lashes out about EU issues on trade and defence; he strongly supported Britain's leaving the EU. Mike Pompeo, Secretary of State in his policy speech in Brussels urged European countries to reassert their sovereignty in relation to the EU. In October or November 2018, EU believes, Trump downgraded their diplomatic status without notice.

Then there is the question of tariffs. US wishes to put car tariffs on imported EU cars, because US says that these imported cars impact adversely on US national security. However EU Commission President Jean-Claude Juncker has told the German Newspaper Stuttgarter Zeitung *that there will be no car tariffs for the time being' because President Trump had given his word on it.* But if tariffs are put on car imports then the EU would respond by stepping back from their commitment to buy soya beans and liquid gas. Trump's words came as a great shock to the EU because until now they have had a harmonious relationship with the US, having so many commonalities. European Union spokesman Margaritis Schinas said that if the U.S. goes ahead with *"actions detrimental to European exports, the European Commission would react in a swift and adequate manner."* German Chancellor Angela Merkel commented that the US had already determined that German cars were a national security threat to the US. That is difficult to comprehend.

Withdrawals and renegotiations – a summary

On January 23, 2017, Trump signed an order to withdraw from further negotiations on the Trans-Pacific Partnership. He promised to replace it with a series of bilateral agreements. As a result, Japan and the EU announced their own trade deal. On July 6, 2017, they agreed to increase Japanese auto exports to the EU and European food exports to Japan.

On August 16, 2017, the Trump administration began renegotiating NAFTA with Canada and Mexico. The North American Free Trade Agreement is the world's largest trade agreement. Trump had threatened to withdraw from NAFTA and hit Mexican imports with a 35 percent tariff.

On September 2, 2017, Trump instructed aides to withdraw from the U.S. trade agreement with South Korea. He wants the country to import more U.S. goods.

On January 22, 2018, Trump imposed tariffs and quotas on imported solar panels and washing machines. On March 1, 2018, he announced a 25 percent tariff on steel imports and a 10 percent tariff on aluminum. Steel users, like automakers, will see higher costs. They will pass that onto consumers. The stock market fell, as analysts correctly forecast that Trump's actions might start a trade war.

On April 3, 2018, Trump announced 25 percent tariffs on $50 billion in Chinese imported electronics, aerospace, and machinery. The administration wants China to stop requiring U.S. companies to transfer their proprietary technology to Chinese firms. They must do this if they want to gain access to China's market. China retaliated hours later. It announced 25 percent tariffs on $50 billion of U.S. exports to China.

On April 6, 2018, Trump announced tariffs on $100 billion more of Chinese imports. It would cover just one-third of U.S. imports from China. If China retaliates, it would impose tariffs on all U.S. exports to China.

On April 10, 2018, China announced that trade negotiations had broken down. The United States demanded that China stop subsidizing the 10 industries prioritized in its "Made in China 2025" plan. Later that day, Chinese President Xi Jinping announced he would reduce tariffs on imported vehicles. Although it allowed Trump to save face, it wouldn't affect trade very much. Most automakers find it is cheaper to build in China, regardless of tariffs.

On May 8, 2018, Trump announced he would withdraw the United States from the Iran nuclear deal.

On May 15, 2018, China agreed to remove tariffs on U.S. pork imports. It will also allow Qualcomm to acquire NXP. In exchange, the United States will remove tariffs on Chinese telecom company ZTE. Many countries see Trump's removal of tariffs on ZTE as a weakness they could exploit. They will redouble efforts to find exceptions to Trump's tariffs. Many European countries want to avoid U.S. sanctions on companies that do business with Iran. They may threaten tariffs on U.S. imports as a bargaining tool.

The Great Depression showed that protectionism doesn't work. Other countries retaliate and international trade declines. Instead of boosting U.S. exports, it will reduce them and increase prices on imports. Even the National Association of Manufacturing wants to expand, not end free trade agreements.

The President quickly ended US participation in the Trans-Pacific Partnership and initiated talks with Canada and Mexico to restructure the North American Free Trade Agreement - negotiations that presently seem to be severely strained.

The US and Canada have also been mired in a dispute over softwood lumber, dairy products and aircraft sales, leading to US "duty investigations" that could lead to new tariffs. In January, Canada filed a formal complaint against the US with the World Trade Organisation, alleging violations of international rules.

Tariffs and Sanctions

Tariff and sanctions have been used by presidents and rulers since ages, often called by other names. But under President Trump it has been taken to new levels against both allies and enemies – from Canada to Iran. Sanctions have been used, generally for foreign policy purposes and tariffs have been used for unfair trading practices. Under Trump they are interchangeable and tariffs are used for foreign policy purposes too. Then too, Trump is using this two-headed hammer without regard and very often. According to Richard Nephew, a senior research scholar at the Center on Global Energy policy and the author of a new book on sanctions says: *Analysts say the White House strategy reflects a fundamental belief in using American economic might to force others to change their behavior, an approach that will test past findings that sanctions often fail absent broad global support.*

Since the 1990's the US has increasingly employed sanctions and tariffs for everything – from human rights violations to terrorism to foreign policy challenges. The differences between before and Trump's use of both is firstly they are used interchangeably and secondly when sanctions are imposed, they are not followed up with any diplomatic move. Both sanctions and tariffs are used extensively, especially by Trump and his son-in-law, Jared Kushner who believe that Kim Jong Un only came to the negotiating table because of sanctions and only through this means can they force Iran and Turkey to make deals. But Iran's foreign minister, Mohammad Javad Zarif disagrees. He said on August 11, 2018 *The US has to rehabilitate its addiction to sanctions and bullying or the entire world will unite – beyond verbal condemnations – to force it to.* Then referring to the tariffs against Turkey, he said: *We've stood with neighbors before and we will again now.* Sanctions have also been placed on Turkey and its interior and justice ministers for refusing to release the Evangelical Pastor Andrew Brunson, (he has since been released as a good gesture). And because Turkey was to acquire a Russian defence system. It would also then show the weakness in the US one.

According to Fred Bergen, the founding director of the Peterson Institute of International Economics the administration's faith that sanctions are a cure all for all foreign policy aims is strongly rooted in its protectionist approach. He also said that *Trump believes that trade barriers are a good policy – having imposed or threatened tariffs against major trading partners such as Canada, China and the European Union.* He also believes that Trump's dislike of committing armed forces overseas is a major part of his *America First approach.* But studies have shown that sanctions and tariffs work between 20-25% of the time and never when it is to force a country to go against what it truly values and/or believes is necessary to its national security like North Korea's Nuclear missile programme. The 213 sanctions on Russian *entities and individuals* and the sanctions imposed on Russia concerning the Ukraine in 2014 also did not change Russia's mind at all. Recently more sanctions were imposed on Russia for <u>allegedly</u> using nerve agent on a former Russian spy. No proof of any kind was proffered. Foreign Ministry Spokeswoman Maria Zakharova said *Russia has repeatedly warned that talking to us from a position of strength and in the language of ultimatums is futile and pointless.* And she continued: *We will consider counter measures to this most recent and unfriendly move by Washington.*

Sanctions have also been imposed on Myanmar over its abuses and humanitarian crimes against the Rohingya Muslim minority of the country. The abuses are still continuing.

Germany was slapped with tariffs on aluminium and steel goods. The German Economy Minister Peter Altmaier criticized Trump's sanctions and tariffs saying they were destroying jobs and growth and that Europe would not bow to US pressure regarding Iran. This triggered a tit-for-tat. The US insisted it was meant to protect US jobs against unfair practices. He also slapped tariffs on China,

EU and other European countries. They retaliated in kind. Trump then decided to put tariffs on EU auto parts but after his meeting with Juncker at the White House, he decided to wait. The US also threatened sanctions and tariffs on any country and entity that had any deals with Iran – after US pulled out of the Iran Deal. Altmaier replied to this by saying it would continue to deal with Iran inspite of US pressure. *"We won't let Washington dictate to us with whom we can do business and we therefore stick to the Vienna Nuclear Agreement so that Iran cannot build atomic weapons,"* Altmaier continued that German companies should be able to invest in Iran as they wished. Several European companies have suspended plans to invest in Iran because of the U.S sanctions, including oil major Total as well as car makers PSA, Renault and Daimler. German business associations said more and more companies are suffering from Trump's sanctions including against Iran and those tariffs in the escalating trade conflict with China.

US Sanctions on the following countries:

Cuba –Trade embargo imposed since 1960 from the time Fidel Castro held power. There is also a travel restriction in place.

Iran- Since 1979 when the Western supported Shah of Iran abdicated/ was deposed and the Iranian hostage crises along with other problems arose, US levied a trade embargo. After the original Iran deal there was a lessening of sanctions but the Trump administration imposed harsher and very severe economic sanctions when the US pulled out of the deal. The US also threatened any country or entity that had dealings with Iran. In June 2019, the US again imposed even harsher sanctions on Iran.

North Korea – a stringent trade embargo has been imposed on the country since 1950 with the Korean ceasefire. It is still continuing. It was and is most brutally affected by the sanctions.

Sudan – Sanctions since 1997

Syria - Since 2004 – Syria has contentious relations with the US. US has imposed very strong restrictions on trade and on financial services. More recently in June 2019 the US sanctioned the export of *League of Legends* (an ebox serial) to Iran and Syria. This is very strange. US says that this is in retaliation for the downing of a US drone over Iranian airspace.

Cöte-d'Ivoire – For human rights violations; trade and arms assistance is prohibited.

Burma (Myanmar) – since 1997 for its human rights violations and for political reasons - a dictatorial regime. US sanctions prohibits US investment, restricts financial services to the ruling party; disallows import of Burmese products and import of US goods. The human violations are continuing, perhaps even worsening, if that is possible.

Russia – Trump has imposed sanctions a number of times on Russia - both corporations and individuals in the public and private sector. Among the many corporations that have been sanctioned, are the Russian public sector assets as well as many individual assets.

Sanctions can also serve to systematically cut off the access of nations, factions within a nation and individuals within a targeted nation from the banks and financial services of the nation levying the sanctions. This has led to sanctioned nations especially China and Russia getting closer while the USA gets left out in the cold.

The US justified levying these sanctions by saying that: they are motivated by *a range of malign activity around the globe,* allegedly conducted by Russia. No proof was forthcoming.

In conclusion, sanctions make the living standard of a country deteriorate sharply. This in turn leads to an economic crisis which in turn leads to mass exodus of economic immigrants to other countries. History says so.

US Tariffs in 2018

China – January on solar panels & washing machines between 30% and 50%. Later in the same year, the US imposed 25% on steel and aluminium 10%. China has accused US of starting a trade war; US levied further tariffs on China and has threatened to add to already existing ones. More sanctions in 2019.

Turkey US put tariffs on steel 25% and on aluminium of 10%. It also put tariffs on the following countries: Canada, India, Australia, EU Mexico, Norway, Russia, Turkey. Some countries were reconsidered and exempted Argentina, Australia, South Korea, Brazil, and Canada. But Robert Lighthizer, the US Trade Representative believes that it is just *a pause* and may only last as long as it takes countries to negotiate or strike new deals. Turkey retaliated by putting tariffs on US coal and paper worth 1.8 billion.

Japan: Has had tariffs imposed on steel (35%) and aluminium (10%). Japan finds this very regrettable and the Japanese Trade Minister Hiroshige Seko says the move is regrettable because as he has mentioned earlier, Japanese steel and aluminium do not pose any national security risk to the US.

India: Was slapped with tariffs on steel, and aluminium and the US also withdrew incentives to Indian exporters under the Generalised system of Preferences (GSP) programme. It was a real surprise when India retaliated by raising tariffs on Whiskey, motorcycles, lentils and other farm products.

Mexico: Due to the US imposition of sanctions and tariffs many US companies have been hit and a lot of workers have lost their jobs. According to Renae Reints (July 5, 2018) the first to be affected was Mid Continental Nail. This Missouri-based company had to let 60 out of its 500 workers go in mid-June 2017 (**Washington Post**). US imports steel from Mexico.

Mexico has been threatened with further crippling tariffs on May 30, 2019.

China: The ongoing trade dispute with China forced REC-Silicon a company that makes solar equipment from imported polysilicon to let 100 of its workers go.

The ongoing tariff increases and sanctions will cause hardship and loss of livelihood to many in the US says the Industry coalition. BMW and General Motors both sent letters to the Commerce Department saying that new tariffs could lead to higher car prices and job cuts at production plants. Volvo had said it would hire 4,000 new employees for a new plant in South Carolina, but it may have to break that commitment as a result of new tariffs.

Harley-Davidson announced it would be moving some of its U.S. production elsewhere after the European Union retaliated by raising U.S. motorcycle tariffs from 6% to 31%, adding nearly $2,200 to the average cost of one of its bikes. The company has not said how many jobs will be affected by this move. U.S. Steel and Century Aluminum have announced it will hire new workers as a result of Trump's tariffs, creating a combined 800 jobs, but this number is dwarfed by the number that could be lost in the coming months. Meanwhile the White House has argued that these tariffs will bring jobs back to the U.S. The U.S. Chamber of Commerce argues in a new campaign that 2.6 million American jobs could be lost as a result of *recent and proposed trade actions by the Trump administration* according to Renae Reints.

Liberalism Threatens The West, Not Iran. This is Why American Liberals Are Wrapping Themselves in The Iranian Flag says Adam Garrie (2018-04-21)

Sanctions and tariffs are imposed when countries are in flagrant violation of accepted rules of behaviour. It is not a tool to use to satisfy the egotistic needs of a leader of a strong state. It can be used successfully when there is a genuine need for its imposition, but when it is used on a whim, arbitrarily and unnecessarily it has the wrong effect.

The US has been targeting not only strong economies and politically strong countries but also small ones – all in the name of US national security interests. It is so far-fetched that it is laughable – for example that a country like South Korea would pose a national security risk to the US especially taking into account the close relationship the two have and all the armed soldiers and weapons of destruction sitting next to South Korea and in South Korea itself.

Since June 2019 new sanctions have been passed on Russian public and private sectors and on Russian private individuals. At the same time more tariffs have been added to the already stiff ones on China. As a consequence it is bringing these two strong nations still closer together – perhaps to be joined by India and maybe even Japan. The point remains that neither has the UN Security Council condemned Russia's malign activities – (no proof of any kind was offered in that case nor it appears, is there any) nor did the WTO find China in violation of its rules. It is strange that instead of promoting peace and harmony - now that the world is relatively stable politically in the sense that no other country besides the US is waging wars around the continents, the US is stirring the pot of discordancy. US, in order to satisfy its ego, is supported by its hanger-ons - some subservient allies who hope to get the crumbs from Trump's table. That will not happen. Trump is only for Trump!

Russia, since the dissolution of the USSR, has successfully managed through diplomacy and its security cooperation initiatives to regain its super power status. China is also a super power through its excellent economic initiatives, industrial production and innovation and its partnerships.

These US sanctions and tariffs can only irritate and anger both these super powers. Both have retaliated in kind. The result of this is lack of trust is a growing suspicion in both China and Russia as to USA's real agenda. It is also further strengthening the Sino-Russian ties. And do not forget they are close neighbours. The USA's bullying tactics have fallen flat.

The Iran Deal

See yonder poor, o'er laboured wight
So abject, mean and vile
Who begs a brother of the earth
To give him leave to toil
And see his lordly fellow worm
The poor petition spurn
Unmindful that a weeping wife
And helpless offspring mourn
Man was made to Mourn by Robert Burns

The 2015 Iran deal or the JCPOA, as it is formally termed, was a landmark agreement between Iran and the world's great powers, including the US. The main reason for this deal was to stop Iran from becoming a nuclear power. It was twelve years in the making. In a recent interview, Germany's Minister of Economic Affairs stated that they (Germany) believed *it can still be seen as an improvement over all other previous deals.* But to President Trump anything initiated by Former President Obama is anathema. Moreover Trump is a strong supporter of Israel as is US State Secretary Mike Pompeo. Benjamin Netanyahu, the Israeli Prime Minister accused (without proof of any kind and against the information of all the other parties to the deal) Iran of lying about its nuclear weapons and stated that those could be activated at any time. Pompeo told reports *I confirm with you, that these documents are real, they are authentic.* This was patently not correct and inspectors had certified Iran's compliance with the deal, most recently in November 2018.

IAEA (International Atomic Energy Agency) said: *Iran is now subject to the world's most robust nuclear verification regime and the IAEA has so far had access to all the locations needed to visit in the country.* So where did Pompeo and Netanyahu get their information from and why did Trump who is very weak towards Israel act arbitrarily on it?

In an effort to reassure Iran, Germany, France and the UK, at the beginning of February 2019, announced a European platform to handle financial transactions not connected with a US-dominated system. They are in the process of registering a company in France with a German official to run the company called the **Instrument in Support of Trade Exchanges**. All three countries will be stakeholders along with the European Union, which is also a signatory to the Iran Peace Deal.

It must be kept in mind that Iran had already made great concessions towards the signing of the peace deal

Among other concessions that Iran agreed to, are:

- To reduce from about 20,000 centrifuges to no more than 6,104 older model centrifuges at only 2 inspected sites. Centrifuges are used to enrich uranium
- To change its Arak heavy water reactor so that reprocessed weapons-grade plutonium could no longer be produced. It could only produce materials for *peaceful medical and industrial nuclear research*
- *Iran agreed to halt uranium enrichment at its Fordow site and convert the site into an isotopic research centre*
- *It agreed to allow international inspections by IAEA of key nuclear facilities to ensure compliance*
- *After signing the Accord it would take Iran at least a year to make a nuclear weapon whereas before the Accord it would have taken the country between two and three months to do so.*

Iran agreed to all this in return for lifting the sanctions and allowing access to the world market, neither of which happened.

US withdrew from the deal in 2018 and reimposed new and harsher sanctions to undermine Iran.

* Highest and toughest sanctions imposed on IRAN

* Any country or company that helps Iran especially with regard to making nuclear weapons will also be severely sanctioned by the US.

The previous sanctions on Iran were lifted in 2015 to help facilitate its economy and allow its oil export. In return Iran accepted restrictions on its nuclear program and allowed international inspectors into the country to inspect its nuclear facilities and to prevent it from acquiring nuclear weapons. This deal was done under President Barack Obama but Trump complained about it that it did not address the ballistic missile programme and nuclear activities beyond 2025 or its participation in the Syrian and Yemeni conflicts. More important still, withdrawing from the Iran deal was one of Trump's election promises.

Withdrawal from this deal will strain US relations with its European allies and disrupt a source of the world's oil supply. It also will allow Iran to expel the international inspectors and resume its nuclear activities.

These new US sanctions will include a broad range of penalties on Iran:

- It will target Iran's oil production and energy institutions
- Its financial institutions
- Its industrial sectors
- Its ability to ensure flow of domestic businesses
- Its access to US dollar commodities and markets

All these to be effective between 90 days and 180 days periods

According to the US Treasury Department, these sanctions are to take effect immediately and any company or entity beginning any business with Iran is to be penalised and refused access to US markets.

Leaders of Britain, France, Germany, Russia and China were signatories of the deal and voiced concern and regret over the US decision but said that they would continue with implementing the deal. Iran, too, intends to remain with the deal.

According to the BBC news there are three main reasons for Trump leaving the Iran Deal:

- His election promise though most Americans weren't too concerned or interested in it
- To shred the Obama legacy because of very personal reasons. He, Trump, has constantly undermined or pulled out of deals made under Obama like
  o the Trans Pacific Partnership (TPP) Trade negotiations;
  o The Paris Accord on climate change
  o Protection for some undocumented immigrants
  o Repealed the Affordable Care Act that under Obama had increased government regulation of health markets
  o Rescinded proposed controls on power-plant emissions
  o Fuel efficiency for some environmental issues
  o Control on some financial institutions.
  o Withdrawal from the Iran-Deal that was one of the highlights of the Obama administration. Concerning this deal Trump had said *I would police that contract so tough that they don't have a chance.* Besides this, withdrawal from this deal was also closely linked to Trump's full-throated support of the Israeli Prime Minister Benjamin Netanyahu. Though Trump professed neutrality in the Arab-Israeli conflict, it was patently not the case.

Trump has also repeatedly criticized Secretary of State under Obama, John Kerry.

In March 2016, Trump told an American-Israeli Public Affairs Conference that his *number one priority is to dismantle the disastrous deal with Iran.*

On February 3rd, 2019 Griff Writte and Eric Cunningham wrote in the Washington Post:

Trump's campaign of choking off American trade to Iran has caused Europe as well as other Islamic countries to suffer. So in retaliation, last week Europe announced unveiling the creation of a trading system to allow firms dealing with Iran to circumvent the US sanctions. But this is not enough in comparison to the US zeal against Iran.

The article also quoted Michael Tockuss, General Secretary of the German-Iranian Chamber of Commerce as saying: *There is more passion from our American friends to create problems.* According to Tockuss, *those problems stem from direct pressure being applied to European firms by US officials, as well as the ripple effect as word spreads and the length to which the Americans will go to force companies to rethink their plans.* Some European companies approached by the US were offered 'friendly' advice to slow down or end their trade deals with Iran. Others were threatened with economic consequences if they failed to comply with US demands.

To the Europeans it is unusual for the US to enforce sanctions so vigorously on the home turf of its closest allies like Germany. But the US did so. The Germans didn't take kindly to this sort of interference. Still, some German companies like Manufacturer Siemens, Allianz, Volkswagen and Daimler have got out. However, companies that do not have very significant trade with the US have continued to stay with the Iran deal. US attacks on these companies have become very aggressive. Finally, US pressure has had very negative and devastating impact on all concerned.

In the end whether this pact will succeed or fail, depends on how hard it hits Iran. At present it has had a strong impact.

This is reflected in EU Council President Donald Tusk who has queried if *US President Donald Trump's recent decisions to go back on several international deals might simply represent temporary frictions in the West's relations, they could also be indicators of the country's new strategy and mark the beginning of the trans-Atlantic breakup (Sputnik, Moscow). He further added that **(the) crucial question today is whether these decisions are only incidental changes to current American policy (to which, of course, every president is entitled) or the beginning of a new strategic trend. Simply put: Are they merely seasonal turbulences or rather the first symptoms of the breakup of the Western political community, which the G-7 represents and informally leads?*** Tusk also emphasized that Trump's decisions had made Europe realise that it is imperative *to protect the trans-Atlantic bond* in spite of their differences and be prepared to act in their own defense. (Moscow – *Sputnik).*

In June 2019 a US military expert claimed that Iran had attacked a Japanese-owned oil tanker *Kokuka Courageous and* a Norwegian *Front Altair* near the Strait of Hormuz. Iran has denied the charge. Now why would Iran attack a Japanese ship and a Norwegian ship? Iran has no quarrel with them. This looks suspiciously like the Racak incidents. There too, experts testified but the testimony had glaring holes in it. Here too there are holes in the statements/assertions. For example the reason for the attack is not given. (Cf. *Betrayal* - by Ashley Smith Chapter on *Racak*).

US Navy Cmdr. Sean Kido, described as an explosives expert, spoke to journalists in Fujairah, a monarchy that makes up the UAE, which has been a leading supporter of Washington's *"maximum pressure campaign"* against Iran. However, he does not give any information as to the make, model, design, distinguishing feature that shows the mine to be of Iranian production.

A former US intelligence officer says it could be Iran but no one *trusts Bolton, Trump, or Pompeo. Lots of bluster and no substance.*

They have also not given the reason for them to investigate an attack on vessels that do not belong to them nor have any connection with the US. They were not carrying US goods.

Even stranger is the connection they are asserting between the explosives used on the ships and the rockets that landed near US facilities in Mosul, Iraq.

In short, according to the Independent (UK) *Iran policy has become so toxic and politicised that it creates an opening for Iran to stage attacks that give Washington hawks just enough reason to accuse Iran, while allowing just enough doubt for critics to accuse them of warmongering.*

Things seem to be getting weirder and weirder and more and more like what happens every time the US decides to bomb a country. The examples are littered through the world's recent history ever since European colonisation of the Americas ended and even earlier.

Both Pompeo and Bolton in Israel and Saudi Arabia and the Gulf States are drumming up support for the bombing of Iran.

Social Issues

Strange Meeting
By <u>Wilfred Owen</u>

Yet also there encumbered sleepers groaned,
Too fast in thought or death to be bestirred.
Then, as I probed them, one sprang up, and stared
With piteous recognition in fixed eyes,
Lifting distressful hands, as if to bless.
And by his smile, I knew that sullen hall,—
By his dead smile I knew we stood in Hell.

"Strange friend," I said, "here is no cause to mourn."
"None," said that other, "save the undone years,
The hopelessness. Whatever hope is yours,
Was my life also;

"I am the enemy you killed, my friend.
I knew you in this dark: for so you frowned
Yesterday through me as you jabbed and killed.
I parried; but my hands were loath and cold.
Let us sleep now. . . ."

Social issues are those which affect human society as a whole. These **issues** pertain to human behavior, including government policies, religious conflicts, gender inequalities, economic disparities, and so on.

They are issues which present a problem or concern that influences a large number of individuals within a society. A social issue has many categories. It is a common problem we see happening in our society and is often the consequence of factors extending beyond an individual's control, and is the source of a conflicting opinion on the grounds of what is perceived as morally correct or incorrect. Social issues are distinguished from economic issues; however, some are distinct but related. The meaning of the term "social issue" (used particularly in the United States) refers to topics of national or political interest, over which the public is deeply divided and which are the subject of intense partisan advocacy, debate, and voting, for example, same-sex marriage and abortion. In this case "social issue" does not necessarily refer to an ill to be solved, but rather to a topic to be discussed. Some issues such as immigration have both social and economic aspects.

Hate crimes are a social problem all over the world because they directly marginalize and target specific groups of people or specific communities based on their identities. Hate crimes can be committed as the result of hate-motivated behavior, prejudice, and intolerance due to sexual orientation, gender expression, biological sex, ethnicity, race, religion, disability etc. Hate crimes, especially in the USA, are a growing issue especially in schools and other educational settings because of the young populations that are part of such institutions. The majority of victims and perpetrators are teenagers and young adults. Hate crimes can result in physical or sexual assaults or harassment, verbal harassment, robbery, or even in death. Trump, the sitting president is fanning hate towards all non-Whites and this can only have serious consequences both in the short and long run. Many White Nationalists and Supremacists are celebrating with the Hitler salute of an extended arm and the slogan "hail Trump." It is also very dangerous because impressionable young people will take from it the carte blanc to behave in a racist manner. School shootings have increased in number and intensity.

I shall look at the very serious social issue of mass shootings, including those which take place in safe places like school, church, synagogue... for whatever the reason. Mass shooting is a very worrying social trend that must be addressed. This particular trend first manifested itself in the Columbine High School massacre of April 20, 1999 where 10 High school students were murdered by two High school students from the same school, one teacher was also killed and then the boys committed suicide. It was a highly sophisticated, well planned and the deadliest before the Stoneman Douglas High School shooting attack of 2018 with the boys using semi-automatic guns, pipe bombs, gasoline bombs, carbine rifles and pump action sawed off shotguns. This incident rocked and shocked the world and set the pattern for future school shootings.

The USA has 46% of the world's guns – not taking into consideration the military hardware but it has 4.27% of the world's population. It has the maximum school shootings in the world. Actually I don't think anywhere else in the world school shooting of this nature and scale takes place. Australia had a school shooting to which the then Prime Minister John Howard responded by buying back all guns and tightening the gun laws. He said: *The greatest civil right is the right to stay alive.* Since then we have not had any other school shooting. Germany, Finland and Scotland also had school shootings but the tightening of gun laws put an end to those too with zero tolerance on school campuses or in the hands of school students. Switzerland has a lot of gun ownership but no school shootings because the background checks are very stringent.

A notable thing here is that countries that have stricter gun laws like New Zealand and Australia do not have this problem to the same extent as countries where guns are easily accessed. When gun toting is part of a culture, accidents and incidents are bound to happen.

Then there is the psychology behind this type of action. A gun in your possession makes you feel invincible, tough and is the answer to all problems. Moreover, when guns are easy to come by and the shooter can have more than one weapon killing is made that much easier and from a distance. Gun violence has become prolific in many countries but most especially in the States where owning guns is not a big deal at all and accessing one is extremely easy. Safety zones are no longer safe but serious death traps. Anyone who has been in violence of any kind, but more especially impressionable students become severely traumatised and often times scarred for life. Some commit suicide. All are scarred in some way – generally psychologically. All public and even private haunts become death traps at any time.

Some of the guns used in shootings at educational institutions with more than 5 fatalities were:

- Hand guns mostly - especially used in close shooting as in the home of family members but also the commonest in all shooting incidents including at educational institutions eg
  o Sandy Hook 28 fatalities
  o Virginnia Tech 32 fatalities
  o Umpqua Community College 10 fatalities
  o Oikos College 7 fatalities
- Semi-automatic guns like the 9mm 67H shotgun used in the
  o Columbine 15 fatalities
- AR-15
  o Marjory Stoneman Douglas 17 fatalities

Statics show handguns are the most popular followed by rifles and then shotguns but whatever the type of gun it usually results in fatalities.

Shootings Jan to April 2019

Date	Location	Fatalities	Wounded	Comments
Jan 1, 2019	Tallahassee, Florida	0	5	shooting in a shopping centre
Jan 1, 2019	Columbia S Carolina	0	5	outside a nightclub
Jan 2, 2019	Jonesboro, Arkansas	1	3	home invasion
Jan 3, 2019	Texas City Texas	3	1	home invasion
Jan 4, 2019	Torrance, California	3	4	in a bowling alley
Jan 4, 2019	Houston Texas	1	3	shooting
Jan 4, 2019	Hurt, Virginia	3	2	Man killed his wife, child injured 2 & shot himself
Jan 6, 2019	Roswell, New Mexico	0	4	at a party – over an argument
Jan 13, 2019	Phoenix, Arizona	1	6	argument in a motel
Jan 15, 2019	Little Rock, Arkansas	1	4	in a local ice-cream shop
Jan 16, 2019	Palmdale California	3	1	shooting
Jan 16, 2019	Jacksonville, Florida	1	5	shooting
Date	**Location**	**Fatalities**	**Wounded**	**Comments**
Jan 17, 2019	Owensboro, Kentucky	3	1	At home
Jan 19, 2019	Houston, Texas	3	2	home invasion
Jan 19, 2019	Chicago, Illinois	0	4	fight (3 women & 1 man)
Jan 19, 2019	Lebanon, Pennsylvania	0	4	targeted shooting
Jan 19, 2019	Jacksonville, Florida	2	3	shooting
Jan 19, 2019	Gaffney, S. Carolina	1	4	at a nightclub
Jan 20, 2019	Miami, Florida	0	4	at a block party
Jan 23, 2019	Sebring, Florida	5	0	Hostage situation
Jan 24, 2019	Rockmart Georgia	4	1	shooting

Jan 24, 2019	State College Pennsylvania	4	1	local bar & home invasion
Jan 26, 2019	Ascension Parish & Livingstone parish, Louisiana	5	0	21-year old targeted both parishes & killed people
Jan 26, 2019	Albany, Georgia	0	4	in front of residence
Jan 26, 2019	Indianapolis, Indiana	0	5	asked to leave a bar; returned with gun & shot customers & staff
Jan 26, 2019	Newark, New Jersey	1	3	at a candlelight vigil
Jan, 27, 2019	Birmingham, Alabama	0	5	shooting
Jan, 28, 2019	Houston, Texas	2	4	4 police officers shot & wounded while serving warrants; 2 perps killed in the exchange
Feb 1, 2019	San Diego, California	0	4	at a house party
Date	**Location**	**Fatalities**	**wounded**	**comments**
Feb 3, 2019	Chicago, Illinois	2	5	a drive-by shooting
Feb 4, 2019	Baton Rouge, Louisiana	0	4	shooting
Feb 4, 2019	Washington D.C.	5	0	bus stop shooting little girl killed along with 4 men
Feb 5, 2019	San Antonio, Texas	2	2	apartment invasion
Feb 6, 2019	Cleveland, Ohio	1	3	neighbourhood shooting
Feb 6, 2019	Brooklyn, New York	1	3	apartment lobby
Feb, 9, 2019	Petersburg, Virginia	0	1	outside an apartment complex
Date	**Location**	**Fatalities**	**Wounded**	**Comments**
Feb 11, 2019	Livingston, Texas	5	0	at home
Feb 14, 2019	Jacksonville, Florida	2	2	at a park; multiple people shot at each other
Feb 15, 2019	Aurora, Illinois	6	6	workplace shooting

Feb 16, 2019	Clinton, Mississippi	5	0	domestic dispute; 12-hr hostage standoff, suspect taken into custody & later died of wounds
Feb 17, 2019	New Orleans, Louisiana	1	5	shooting
Feb 17, 2019	Henderson, Texas	2	2	apartment complex shooting
Feb 17, 2019	Evansville, Indiana	0	5	outside a bar
Feb 18, 2019	Solon Township, Michigan	4	0	28-year-old woman shot her children & herself
Feb 20, 2019	Covington, Tennessee	0	4	home shooting
Feb 21, 2019	Houston, Texas	2	2	From a rooftop at home – following an argument he shot others
Feb 21 2019	Baltimore, Maryland	1	4	shooting
Feb 21 2019	Elizabethtown, Kentucky	2	2	same man 2 shootings
Feb 22, 2019	Birmingham, Alabama	2	2	at a party at home
Feb 28, 2019	Oakland, California	1	4	Shooting near a gas station
March 2, 2019	Pine Bluff, Arkansas	1	4	at a party at home
March 3, 2019	Chicago, Illinois	0	6	bar shooting
March 3, 2019	Oakland, California	0	4	sports bar shooting
March 10, 2019	Shreveport, Louisiana	0	4	Drive-by shooting
March 10, 2019	Denver, Colorado	1	4	Conflict between 2 led to this shooting
March 11, 2019	Paterson, New Jersey	0	4	shooting in a liquor store
March 13, 2019	Harvey, Illinois	1	3	Nightclub

Date	Location	Fatalities	Wounded	Comments
March 14, 2019	Missoula, Montana	1	3	road rage incident
March 15, 2015	Mobile, Alabama	2	3	overnight shooting behind a home
March 16, 2019	Camden, New Jersey	1	3	'residential speakeasy" shooting
March 17, 2019	Rochelle, Georgia	1	3	dispute led to shooting
March 17, 2019	Las Vegas, Nevada	0	4	Hotel & Casino shooting
March 17, 2019	Augusta, Georgia	0	4	random attack – shooter claimed, so he shot them
March 19, 2019	Phoenix, Arizona	2	4	house party
March 24, 2019	Phoenix, Arizona	0	7	warehouse party
March 24, 2019	San Francisco, California	1	5	near Fillmore Heritage Center
March 25, 2019	North Las Vegas, Nevada	0	5	after school fight – teenage shooting
March 28, 2019	Baltimore, Maryland	0	4	shooting near a playground
March 31, 2019	North Charleston, South Carolina	0	7	overnight house party
Date	**Location**	**Fatalities**	**Wounded**	**Comments**
March 31, 2019	Atlanta, Georgia	4	1	2men & 2 women died at 2 locations
March 31, 2019	Chicago, Illinois	5	5	at a manufacturing company 5 police wounded
April 2, 2019	Covington, Kentucky	0	5	drive-by shooting
April 2, 2019	Hermanville, Mississippi	0	4	drive by shooting
April 4, 2019	Stockbridge, Georgia	3	2	hostage situation; murder-suicide
April 4, 2019	Panama City, Florida	1	3	shooter a security guard
April 6, 2019	Talahassee, Florida	0	4	students; at a house party

April 6, 2019	Chicago, Illinois	0	6	shooting at a baby shower
April 7, 2019	Wilmington, Delaware	0	6	street shooting
April 7, 2019	Shreveport, Louisiana	0	4	in a mobile home park
April 7, 2019	Indianapolis, Indiana	2	3	at a motorcycle club
April 7, 2019	Winston-Salem North Carolina	0	6	shooting outside a local bar
April 9, 2019	Kansas City, Missouri	0	4	found with gunshot wounds in front of residence
April 11, 2019	Baltimore, Maryland	1	3	Shooting perpetrator arrested
April 11, 2019	Los Angeles, California	1	4	guns fired from moving car
Date	**Location**	**fatalities**	**wounded**	**Comments**
April 11, 2019	Phoenix, Arizona	3	0	Man killed his wife & 2 daughters 1 with blunt force trauma & 2 by shooting
April 12, 2019	Carbondale, Illinois	0	4	shooting outside of a Restaurant & bar
April 14, 2019	Miami, Florida	2	2	Drive by shooting
April 14, 2019	Stockton California	0	4	man opened fire inside bar
April 14, 2019	Vallejo, California	1	3	early morning shooting
April 16, 2019	Germantown, Maryland	1	3	drive by shooting
April 18, 2019	Louisville, Kentucky	0	4	one car shot at another & injured 4
April 19, 2019	Wichita, Kansas	0	4	at a party
April 20, 2019	Corpus Christi, Texas	0	4	disturbance escalated to violence (shooting)
April 20, 2019	Memphis, Tennessee	0	7	in a fight

Date	Location	Fatalities	Wounded	Comments
April 21, 2019	Los Angeles, California	0	4	4 senior citizens were wounded when the car behind them opened fire. Motive unknown
April 21, 2019	Philadelphia, Pennsylvania	0	4	
April 27, 2019	Poway Synagogue, California	1	3	Shooter: John Earnest 19 An off-duty cop inside the synagogue shot at the suspect. Later picked up by highway patrol
Date	Location	Fatalities	Wounded	Comments
April 27, 2019	Westmoreland, Tennessee	7	2	2 separate locations Killer was a 25-year-old man
April 27, 2019	Jackson, Mississippi	0	4	overnight shooting
April 27, 2019	Jackson, Mississippi	1	3	shooting in South Jackson
April 28, 2019	Baltimore, Maryland	1	7	Gunman opened fire on 2 cookouts at an intersection
April 28, 2019	Birmingham, Alabama	0	4	Suspect in a vehicle opened fire on patrons outside a nightclub
April 28, 2019	Nashville, Tennessee	0	7	Altercation at a party led to gunshots & others got injured in the crossfire
April 28, 2019	West Chester Township, Ohio	4	0	4 family members found shot dead. Suspect not apprehended
Date	Location	Fatalities	Wounded	Comments
May 1, 2019	Boston, Massachusetts	1	3	Victims were attacked while sitting in a parked car
May 3, 2019	Dallas, Texas	1	3	Victims of a drive-by shooting

date	location	fatalities	wounded	comments
May 3, 2019	Baltimore, Maryland	0	5	Emergency responders found 1 female, 2 males 2 kids all same incident
May 3, 2019	Baltimore, Maryland	0	4	shot spotter gunfire alert notified police of incident
May 4, 2019	Wilmington, Delaware	0	4	Shooting at West 27th & Tatnall Streets
May 4, 2019	Indianapolis, Indiana	0	4	3 teens & a man in a fight among 20-30 people
May 4, 2019	Saint Louis, Missouri	1	4	All 5 victims shot inside a vehicle. 1 died
May 5, 2019	Oceano, California	0	6	Police responded to call. Transferred wounded to hospital
May 5, 2019	North Bergen, New Jersey	1	4	a fight escalated
date	**location**	**fatalities**	**wounded**	**comments**
May 7, 2019	Stem School Highlands Ranch, Colorado	1	8	2 suspects in custody
May 8, 2019	Indianapolis, Indiana	0	4	shooting
May 10, 2019	Philadelphia, PA	0	5	3 teenage boys
May 10, 2019	St Louis, Missouri	0	6	shooting
May 11, 2019	Chestnuthill, PA	0	4	shooter arrested
May 11, 2019	Paulsboro, New Jersey	0	4+1	shooting
May 13, 2019	New Orleans Louisiana	0	4	Drive by shooting
May 13, 2019	St. Louis Missouri	4	1	home shooting
May 15, 2019	St. Rose, Louisiana	0	4	altercation
May 16. 2019	Cleveland, Ohio	0	4	shooting
May 17 2019	Sacramento CA	1	4	targeted shooting
May 18, 2019	Muncie, Indiana	0	7	house party
May 18, 2019	Winston-Salem, North Carolina	1	5	overnight block party
May 18, 2019	Long Beach, CA	1	5	vigil in local bar shooting

Date	location	fatalities	wounded	comments
May 18, 2019	Atmore, Alabama	1	8	high school graduation party
May 18, 2019	Cedar Rapids, Iowa	2	2	shots fired into vehicle outside a tobacco store
May 18, 2019	Cascilla, Mississippi	1	5	family dispute shooting
May 19, 2019	Portland, Oregon	0	5	warehouse party
May 20, 2019	Tulsa, Oklahoma	2	2	apartment complex
May 20, 2019	Columbus, Ohio	0	4	shooting
May20, 2019	Alexandria, Louisiana	1	4	shooting
May 25, 2019	Trenton, New Jersey	0	10	bar shooting
May25, 2019	Chesapeake, Virginia	1	9	shooting at a party
May 25, 2019	Oklahoma city, Oklahoma	0	5	parking lot shooting
Date	**location**	**fatalities**	**wounded**	**comments**
May 25, 2019	Baltimore, Maryland	0	4	found lot in park
May 26, 2019	Chicago, Illinois	2	3	shooting at a party
May 26, 2019	Washington, D.C.	1	3	shooting in parking lot
May 26, 2019	La Crosse, Virginia	0	5	multiple shooter Block party
May 26, 2019	Stockton, California	1	3	shooting
May 27, 2019	Washington D.C.	0	5	shooting
May 27, 2019	Trenton, New Jersey	1	5	shooting on Walnut Ave.
May 29, 2019	Cleveland, Texas	2	3	shooting at plumbing company
May 30. 2019	Robbins, Illinois	0	5	vehicle pulled up and opened fire
May 31, 2019	Virginia Beach, Virginia	13	4	city public works building.
June 1, 2019	Macon, Georgia	0	4	shooting – block party
June 1, 2019	Allendale, S. Carolina	0	5	shooting - carwash
June 1, 2019	Atlanta, Georgia	0	5	shooting
June 1, 2019	Chicago, Illinois	1	3	shooting

June 1, 2019	Chicago, Illinois	0	4	Shooting
June 1, 2019	Portsmouth, Virginia	1	3	overnight shooting
June 5, 2019	Santa Rosa, Calif.	0	4	teenager shot others at soccer park
June 6, 2019	Chicago, Illinois	1	3	shooting from 1 vehicle to another
June 7, 2019	Austin, Texas	0	5	shooting
June 8, 2019	Chicago, Illinois	0	4	shooting after altercation
June 8, 2019	White Swan, Washington	5	0	Shooting in Indian Reservation. Suspect at large.
date	**location**	**fatalities**	**wounded**	**comments**
June 9, 2019	Cleveland, Ohio	1	3	shooting on crowd in Kerruish Park
June 9, 2019	Buffalo, New York	0	4	shooting – after a dispute
June 9, 2019	Henning, Tennessee	1	3	Shooting in a nightclub
June 11, 2019	Aurora, Colorado	0	4	overnight shooting
June 11, 2019	Savannah, Georgia	2	2	
June12, 2019	Charlotte, North Carolina	1	3	shooting – at a party
June 15, 2019	West Des Moines, Iowa	4	0	gun shot – in a house
Date	**Location**	**Fatalities**	**Wounded**	**Comments**
June 15, 2019	Shreveport, Louisiana	0	4	drive by shooting outside a nightclub
June 16, 2019	Des Moines, Iowa	0	6	drive-by shooting in a street
June16, 2019	Louisville, Kentucky	1	6	shot near a liquor store
June 16, 2019	Philadelphia, Pennsylvania	1	7	graduation party -teenagers
June 17, 2019	Memphis, Tennessee	0	5	parking lot of apartment complex
June 17, 2019	San Antonio, Texas	0	4	gunfire, altercation with another motorist
June 18, 2019	Newark, New Jersey	1	6	gunfire - downtown

Date	Location	fatalities	Wounded	Comments
June20, 2019	Allentown, Pennsylvania	0	10	gunfire outside a nightclub
June21, 2019	Chicago, Illinois	0	4	shooting - apartment complex
June 21, 2019	Richmond, California	0	5	drive by shooting
June 21, 2019	Saginaw, Michigan	1	3	shot in the house
June 22, 2019	Baltimore, Maryland	1	4	gunman fired on a crowd
June 22, 2019	Hampton, Virginia	0	4	shooting Buckroe Beach
June 22, 2019	Philadelphia, Pennsylvania	0	4	overnight shooting
June23, 2019	South Bend, Indiana	1	10	shooting at a local bar
June23, 2019	La Jolla, California	1	3	drive by shooting at a party
Date	**Location**	**fatalities**	**Wounded**	**Comments**
June 23, 2019	Columbus, Ohio	0	5	drive by shooting outside a motorcycle shop
June 23, 2019	Abbeville South Carolina	3	1	shooting apt. complex
June 23, 2019	San Jose, California	5	0	4-hour standoff then shooting
June 26, 2019	Akron, Ohio	1	3	shooting – home invasion
June 27, 2019	Atlanta, Georgia	0	7	Drive by shooting
June 28, 2019	Hamden, Connecticut	0	5	shooting house party
June 28, 2019	Paterson, New Jersey	0	4	street shooting
June 28, 2019	Atlanta, Georgia	0	7	drive by shooting
June 29, 2019	Chicago, Illinois	05	5	gunfire at a gathering
June 29, 2019	Hartford, Connecticut	0	4	
June 29, 2019	Baton Rouge, Louisiana	0	7	shooting outside a nightclub
June 30, 2019	Bay Shore New York	0	6	shooting – house party

June 30, 2019	Dallas, Texas	2	2	drive by shooting near a playground
June 30, 2019	Yucaipa, California	0	5	mobile home after a BBQ
	Oakland, California			

Month	total incidents	fatalities	wounded	Comments
January 2019	28	46	86	all shooting incidents
February 2019	22	41	65	all shooting incidents
March 2019	21	14	89	all shooting incidents
April 2019	**53**	**32**	**126**	**all shooting incidents & 1 blunt force trauma**
May 2019	**43**	**40**	**197**	**all shooting**
June 2019	**49**	**42**	**113**	**all shooting**

Conclusion:

From the above chart for the first half of this year 2019, it is clear that frequency of incidents is increasing with the peak in April but the highest fatalities were in June. This is not taking into account school shootings or shootings in other educational institutions. Gun offences are also the commonest. No place is safe – not the home, not at a party or the playground or at a nightclub or even the street. Another thing to note is that you do not need to have a quarrel with the shooter to get shot. Everyone, everywhere is at risk and the gun is the preferred weapon. Death and injury stalk the innocent bystander and inmates of the home as well as those with whom they might have some issue.

Highest incidents in April 2019 all but 1 gun violence
Highest fatalities in June
Largest number of wounded was in May.
So, April, May and June all showed a peaking of danger.

Mass Shootings

Mass shooting is generally regarded as the attack on more than 2 people by the perpetrator (s). In the 1980's the US FBI defined it as the killing of 4 or more people in a single incident (excluding himself), in one specific location (Krouse & Richardson 2015). There is no one universally accepted definition. In this paper I have considered an attack on two or more people as mass shootings. This part deals with the total aggregates for the different years between 2010 and 2019. The information is based on previous research (see Mass shooting websites).

Year	Month	Killed	Injured	total
2019	June	42	113	155
	May	**40**	**197**	**237**
	APRIL	18	103	121
	MARCH	28	85	113
	Feb	38	72	110
	Jan	47	86	133
2018	Nov	18	21	39
	Oct	12	13	25
	Sept	8	5	13
	Aug	3	9	12
	June	11	24	35
	May	10	14	24
	April	4	2	6
	March	5	0	5
	Feb	17	17	34
	Jan	2	16	18
2017	Dec	5	6	11
	Nov	33	32	65
Las Vegas	**Oct**	**59**	**851**	**910**
	Sept	10	9	19
	Aug	2	4	6
	July	0	28	28
	June	18	13	31

Year	Month	Fatalities	Injured	total
	May	8	1	9
	April	7	1	8
	March	7	16	23
	Jan	5	6	11
2016	Sept	7	3	10
	Aug	6	0	6
	July	16	17	33
	June	**50**	**103**	**153**
	May	3	3	6
	April	8	0	8
	March	6	3	9
	Feb	10	16	26
2015	Dec	16	22	38
	Nov	3	14	17
	Oct	10	8	18
	Aug	8	0	8
	July	9	10	19
	June	9	1	10
	May	9	18	27
	Feb	8	1	9
2014	Dec	6	5	11
	Oct	5	1	6
	July	6	1	7
	May	7	13	20
	April	7	14	21
Year	**Month**	**Fatalities**	**Injured**	**total**
2013	Nov	1	4	5
	Sept	13	8	21
	Aug	3	4	7
	July	7	0	7
	June	6	5	11
	Feb	5	7	12
	Jan	5	0	5
2012	Dec	28	2	30
	Aug	9	13	22
	July	12	70	82
	April	7	3	10

	Feb	3	3	6
2011	Nov	5	1	6
	Oct	8	1	9
	Sept	9	7	16
	July	8	2	10
	Jan	6	15	21
2010	Aug	9	2	11
	Feb	3	3	6
	Jan	12	5	17

year	fatalities	total	comments
2019	136	612	Until May
2018	90	211	
2017	316	1283	LasVegas shooting
2016	106	142	
2015	72	152	
2014	31	65	
2013	40	68	
2012	**59**	**150**	**Sandy Hook school**
2011	36	62	
2010	24	34	

Mass shooting peaked in 2017, 2018 was the worst and 2019 – all during the Trump presidency when gun laws were loosened.

Shootings at Educational Institutions

According to the web site https://www.presstv.com/Detail/2019/03/24/591817/US-school-shooting-survivors-commit-suicide On 23 March 2019 a sophomore student who had survived the Marjory Stoneman Douglas High School shooting of Feb 2019 in which 17 students were killed, committed suicide due to post traumatic shock and was followed by another student from the same school for the same reason. As I mentioned earlier, the effects of being in a shooting has far-reaching consequences on the witnesses. These deadly and meaningless acts of violence are corroding the very fabric of social and civic values as well as that of life itself.

This is a list of school shootings between 1985 and 2019

Date	School	Fatalities	Wounded	Shooter
Jan 21 1985	Goddard Junior High School (Kansas)	1(Principal)	32 teachers & 1 student	James Alan Kearby age 14 years
Oct 18, 1985	Murray Wright High School (Detroit)	0	6	an youth fired on football team
Nov 26,1985	Spanaway High School- (Washington)	3 including shooter	0	Heather Smith in the school gym
Dec 3, 1985	Concord High School (New Hampshire)	1	0	Louis Cartier16 yrs.; police shot him
Dec 10, 1985	Portland Junior High school (Connecticut)	1	2	Floyd Warmsley 13 years old
Mar 6, 1986	Thornridge High School (Illinois)	0	1	a freshman student
April 29, 1986	Hornersville High School (Missouri)	1	0	Ritchie Overman

May 9, 1986	Pine Forest High School (North Carolina)	0	1	17 year old student
May 16, 1986	Cokeville Elementary School (Wyoming)	2 (both shooters)	74 (1by gunfire)	David Young 47 & Doris his wife
Dec 4 1986	Fergus High School (Montana)	1	3	Kristofer Hans
Feb 4, 1987	California State University (Northridge)	2 including the shooter - suicide	0	Fawwaz Abdin 25 years old

Year	School	Fatalities	Wounded	Shooter
March 2, 1987	DE Kalb (Missouri)	2 including shooter	0	Nathan Ferris 12 years old
April 16, 1987	Murray-Wright High School (Michigan)	1	2	a ninth grade student
Sept 28, 1987	Illiana Christian School (Illinois)	0	1	Blake Docter 16 years old
Feb 11, 1988	Pinellas Park High School (Florida)	1	2	Jason Harless & Jason McCoy both 15 years old
May 20 1988)	Hubbard Woods School (Illinois	1committed suicide later	5	Lauri Dann 30 years old
July 10, 1988	Siefert Elementary School (Wisconsin)	0	1	28 year old man
Sept 22, 1988	Moses Montefort Academy (Illinois)	5 including the shooter	2	Clemmie Henderson 40 years old
Sept 26, 1988	Oakland Elementary School (SouthCarolina)	2	9	William Wilson 19 years old
Nov 22, 1988	Cooper High School (Texas)	0	1	Mason Staggs 16 years old
Dec 16, 1988	Atlantic Shores Christian School (Virginia)	1	1 (gun jammed)	Nicholas Elliott 16 years old

Jan 17, 1989	Stockton Schoolyard/ Cleveland Elementary School California	6 including shooter	32	Patrick Edward Purdy 24 years old
Feb 10, 1989	Thomas Jefferson Junior High School (Utah)	0	0	12 year-old boy
Dec 5, 1989	Serra Catholic High School (Pennsylvania)	1 (the shooter)	1	Robert Butler 16 years old
March 27, 1990	Public school in Bensonhurst, Brooklyn (NY)	0	1	3 White boys shot a black boy
Sept 11, 1990	Sam Houston High School (Texas)	0	3	18 year-old Kenneth Wolford a & 2 more boys
April 23, 1991	Ralph J Bunche Middle School (California)	1	0	a teenager
Sept 18, 1991	Crosby High School (Texas)	1	0	LaKeeta Cadoree 15 years old

Date	School	Fatalities	Wounded	Shooter
Nov 1, 1991	University of Iowa	6 including shooter	1	Gang Lu 28 years old
Nov 25, 1991	Thomas Jefferson High School (New York)	1	0	Jason Bentley 14 years old
Jan 29, 1992	Kent State University (Ohio)	0	1	
Feb 26, 1992	Thomas Jefferson High School second shooting	2	0	Kahlil Sumpter 15 years old
March 5, 1992	Hamilton Midle School (Ohio)	0	1	Gordon W. Dye Jr
April 23, 1992	Indiana University (Indiana)	3 including shooter	0	ex boyfriend

Date	School	Fatalities	Wounded	Shooter
May 1, 1992	Lindhurst High School (California)	4	10	Fmr. student Eric Houston 20 years old
September 11, 1992	Paulo Duro High School (Texas)	0	7	Randy Earl Matthews 17 years old
Oct 19, 1992	BronxHigh School (New York)	0	3	
Nov 4, 1992	Finney High School (Michigan)	0	11	3 separate incidents
Dec 14, 1992	Bard College at Simon's Rock (Massachuetts	2	4	Wayne Lo Taiwanese born American
Jan 6, 1993	Brentwood High School (New York)	0	1	2 gunmen
Jan 18, 1993	East Carter High School (Kentucky)	2	0	Scott Pennington 17 years old
Feb 22, 1993	Reseda High School (LA, California)	1	0	Robert Heard 15 years old
April 15, 1993	Ford Middle School ((Massachuetts	1	0	David Taber 44 years old not guilty due to insanity
May 14, 1993	Nimitz High School (Texas)	1	0	Max Alexander Martinez 17 years old
May 24, 1993	Upper PerkiomenHigh School (Pennsylvania	1	0	Jason Smith 15 years old
Sept 17,	Central Junior High School	1 shooter suicide	4	Kevin Newman 29 years old

Date	School	Fatalities	Wounded	Shooter
Nov 4, 1993	New Britain High School	1	0	Maurice Flanagan & Thomas Mejia 23 years old 24 years old

Date	Institution	Killed	Wounded	Shooter
Dec 1, 1993	Wauwatosa West High School (Wisconsin)	1	0	Leonard D. McDowell 21 –year-old former student
Jan 24, 1994	Eau Claire High School (S. Carolina)	1	0	Floyd Eugene Brown 18 years old
Jan 31, 1994	Whitman Middle School (Seattle, Washington)	1	0	Darrell Cloud 24 years old
Feb 18, 1994	Spartanburg High School (S. Carolina)	0	1	
March 1, 1992	Kemper Military School (Missouri)	2	0	Dante D Hayes 33 years old
April 12, 1994	Margaret Leary Elementary School (Montana)	1	0	Jason Osmanson 10 years old teased because his parents had AIDS
April 21, 1994	J.T. Moore Middle School (Tennessee	1	0	Jeremy Bryant 14 years old
October 12, 1994	Grimsley High School (North Carolina)	1 himself (suicide)	1	Nicholas Atkinson 16 years old
October 17, 1994	Hubbard High School Illinois)	0	1	teenage boy riding past
November 7, 1994	Wickliffe Middle School (Ohio)	1	5 including shooter	Keith A Ledeger 37 year old school custodian
December 14, 1994	State University of New York	0	1	Ralph J Tortorici
January 12, 1995	Garfield High School (Washington)	0	2	a 15-year old student
Sept 29, 1995	Tavares Middle School (Florida)	1	0	Keith E. Johnson
Oct 12, 1995	Blackville Hilda High School (S Carolina)	2 including shooter	1	(suspended) Toby R. Sincino 16 years old)
Nov 15, 1995	Richland High School (Tennessee)	2	1	James Rouse 17 years old

Jan 19, 1996	Winston Education Center (Washington D.C.)	3	1	16 yearDarrick Evans & another man both masked
Year	**School name**	**fatalities**	**wounded**	**shooter's name**
Feb 2, 1996	Frontier Middle School (Washington)	3	1	Barry Loukaitis 14 years old
Feb 29 1996	On bus to Beaumont High School (Missouri)	2	1	Mark Boyd (30) hired Malik Nettles (23) to kill Kyunia Taylor (15). Pregnant with Boyd's child
Aug 15, 1996	San Diego State University	3	0	Frederick Martin Davidson ((36) graduate student
Sept 17,1996	Pennsylvania State University (Pennyslavania)	1	2	Jillian Robbins (19)
Sept 25 1996	Dekalb Alternative School (Georgia)	1	2	David Dubose Jr. (16) mentally unsound
Oct 9 1996	On bus toWiley Hall dorm (Layfayette, Indiana)	2 including shooter	0	Jarrod Allan Eskew (18)
Jan 27, 1997	Conniston Middle School (Florida)	1	0	Tronnel Magnum (14)
Feb 19, 1997	Bethel Regional High School(Alaska)	2	2	Evan Ramsey(16)
Oct 1, 1997	Pearl High School (Mississippi)	3	7	Luke Woodhman (16) killed mother, girlfriend & another girl
Oct 15, 1997	Lincoln Middle School (Florida)	0	1	Brandon Hartsoe (13)

Date	School	Fatalities	Wounded	Shooter
Dec 1, 1997	Heath High School (Kentucky)	3	5	Michael Carneal (14) killed other students at prayers
Dec 15, 1997	Stamps High School (Arkansas	0	2	Joseph "Colt" Todd (14)
March 1, 1998	After basketball game near Pennsylvania Uni.	1	3	
March 24, 1998	Westside Middle School (Arkansas)	5	10	Mitchell Johnson (13) & Andrew Golden (11)
April 24, 1998	Parker Middle School (Pennsylvania)	1	3	Andrew Wurst (14)
May 19, 1998	Lincoln County High School (Tennessee)	1	0	Jacob Lee Davies (18)May 21, 1998
May 21, 1998	shooter's home & Thurston High School (Oregon)	4	25	Kip Kinkel (15) killed his parents then killed at school
June 15, 1998	Armstrong High School (Virginia)	0	2	Quinshawn Brooker (14)
Year	**School**	**Fatalities**	**Wounded**	**Shooter**
Dec 190, 1998	Wayne State Uni. (Michigan)	1	0	Doctoral student Wlodzimierz Dedecjusat (48)
Jan 8, 1999	Central Carrolton County High School	2 (both shooters)	0	Andrea Garrett (15) & Jeff Miller (17) suicide pact
April 16, 1999	Notus Jr. Sr. High School (Idaho)	0	0	Shawn Cooper (15) suffered from Bipolar

April 20, 1999	Columbine High School (Colorado)	15 including both shooters	21	Eric Harris (18) & Dylan Klebold (17) Planned in advance firearms, sawed-off shotgun, pipe bombs etc.
May 20, 1999	Heritage High School (Georgia)	0	6	Thomas "TJ" Solomon Jr.(15) Mental illness
Nov 19. 1999	Deming Middle School (New Mexico)	1	0	Victor Cordova Jr. (13)had intended to commit suicide Jostled & missed, hit another
Dec 6, 1999	Fort Gibson Middle School (Oklahoma)	0	6	Seth Trickey (13) Brought gun from home
Date	**location**	**fatalities**	**wounded**	**shooter**
Feb 29, 2000	Buell Elementary School (Michigan)	1	0	Dedrick Owens (6) Youngest documented shooter
May 26, 2000	Lake Worth Middle School (Florida)	1	0	Nathaniel Brazill (13)
June 28, 2000	Uni Of Washington Medical Center	2 (including shooter)	0	Jian Cham (42) non-renewal of contract
Aug 28, 2000	Uni of Arkansas (Arkansas)	2 (including shooter)	0	James Easton Kelly (36) dismissed from Ph D prog.
Sept 26, 2000	New Orleans Louisiana	0	2	Darell Johnson(13) &Alfred Anderson(13)
Date	**Location**	**Fatalities**	**Wounded**	**Shooter**

Dec 1, 2000	Junipero Serra High School	0	1 (boy with gun)	A 15 year old brought handgun to school and accidentally shot himself
March 5, 2001	Santana High School (California)	2	13	Charles Andrew Williams (15)
March 7, 2001	Bishop Neuman High School	0	1	Elizabeth Catherine Bush (14)
March 22, 2001	Granite Hills High School (California)	0	5	Jason Hoffman (18.) committed suicide in prison
March 30, 2001	outside Lew Wallace High School	1	0	Donald Ray Burt Jr. (17)
May 16, 2001	Pacific Lutheran University (Washington)	2 including the shooter	0	A man from Tacoma (aged 55) not of the Uni.
Jan 15,2002	Martin Luther King Jr. High School (NY City NY)	0	2	Vincent Rodriguez (17)
Jan 16, 2002	Appalachian School of Law (Virginia)	3	3	Peter Odighizuwa (42)
Feb 20, 2002	Washington High School (Wisconsin)	1	0	Philip D. Jackson Jr.
Oct 7, 2002	Benjamin Tasker Middle School Maryland) – Beltway sniper attacks	1	0	Lee Boyd Malvo & John Allen Muhammad
Oct28, 2002	Uni. of Arizona (Arizona)	4 including shooter	0	Robert Stewart Flores Jr. (40) Oct 29, 2002
Oct 29, 2002	Lincoln High School (New Jersey)	0	1	?

Date	Location	fatalities	wounded	shooter
April 14, 2003	John McDonogh High School (Louisiana)	1	3	Steven Williams (18) & James Tate (17)
April 24, 2003	Red Lion Junior High School (Pennsylvania)	2 including shooter	0	James Shee4ts (14)
May 9, 2003	Case Western Reserve Uni. (Ohio)	1	2	Biswanath Halder (62) Also held campus hostage for 7 hrs until SWAT team arrived
Sept 24, 2003	Rocori High School (Minnesota)	2	0	John Jason McLaughlin (15)
Feb 2, 2004	Ballou HighSchool (Washington DC)	1	0	Thomas J Boykin (
Feb 9, 2004)	East Greenbush,(NY	0	1	John W Romano
Date	**Location**	**fatalities**	**wounded**	**shooter**
May 7, 2004	Randallstown High School (Maryland)	0	4	2 students charged with the shooting
Feb 8, 2005	Bowen High School (Illinois)	0	1	?
March 2, 2005	Dover, (Tennessee)	1	0	Jason Clinard (14) shot his bus driver on pick up to school
March 21, 2005	Red Lake Senior High School (Minnesota)	10 including shooter	7	Jeffry Weise(16) first killed grandfather & his companion
Sept. 13, 2005	Harlan Community Academy High School Chicago, Illinois)	0	1	Christopher Huff (15)
Nov 8, 2005	Campbell County High School (Tennessee)	1	2	Kenneth Bartley (15)
Feb 23, 2006	Roseburg High School (Oregon)	0	1	Vincent Wayne Leodoro (14)

Date	Location	fatalities	wounded	shooter's name
March 14, 2006	Pine Middle School (Nevada)	0	2+2 received minor wounds	James Scott Newman (14)
Aug 24, 2006	Essex Elementary School (Vermont)	2	3 (including shooter himself)	Christopher Williams (26)
Aug 30, 2006	Hillsborough, North Carolina	1	2	Alvaro Castillo (teenager) obsessed with Columbine killings)
Sept 2, 2006	Shepard Uni. (West Virginia	3 (including shooter)	0	Douglas W Pennington (49)
Sept 17, 2006	Pittsburg (Pennsylvania)	0	5	?
Sept 27, 2006	Platte Canyon High School (Colorado)	2(including shooter)	0	Duane Roger Morrison (59) drifter
Sept 29, 2006	Weston High School (Wisconsin)	1	0	Eric Hainstock (15) had shotgun & revolver with him
Oct 6, 2006	Nickel Mines School (Pennsylvania)	6 (including Shooter)	5	Charles Carl Robert IV (32)
Oct 9, 2006	Memorial Middle School (Missouri)	0	0	Thomas White (13) fired repeatedly at the principal but failed
Jan 3, 2007	Henry Foss High School (Washington)	1	0	Douglas S. Chanthaboul (18)
Date	**Location**	**fatalities**	**wounded**	**shooter**
March 7, 2007	Centennial High School (California)	0	1	?

Date	Location	Fatalities	Wounded	Shooter
April 16, 2007	**Virginia Tech (Virginia)**	**33 (including shooter**	**23**	Seung Hui Cho (23) 2 separate attacks Third deadliest shooting by a lone person in modern US history
Sept 21, 2007	Delware State University (Delware)	1	1	Loyer D Braden?
Oct 10, 2007	Success Tech Alternative High School (Ohio)	1(Shooter)	5	Asa H Coon (14)
Feb 4, 2008	Hamilton High School (Tennessee)	0	1	a student
Feb 8, 2008	Louisiana Technical College (Lousiana)	3 (including shooter)	0	Latina Williams (23) nursing student
Feb 11, 2008	Miami Carol City Senior High School (Florida)	01	1	Patrick Lively(19)
Feb 11, 2008	Mitchell High School (Tennessee)	0	1	sophomore student (17)
Feb 12, 2008	E.O. Green Junior High School (California)	1	0	Brandon McInerney (14) Feb 14, 2008
Feb 14, 2008	Northern Illinois University (Illinois)	6 (including shooter)	21	Steven Kazmierczak (21)
Aug 14, 2008	Lakota Middle School (Washington)	1	0	Luis F. Cosgaya-Alvarez
Aug 21, 2008	Central High School (Tennessee)	1	0	Jamar Siler (15)
Sept 2, 2008	South High School (Ohio)	0	0	an unnamed student
Date	**Location**	**Fatalities**	**Wounded**	**Shooter**
Oct 16, 2008	Henry Ford High school (Michigan)			William Morton (15) Devon Bell & another student

Date	Institution	Killed	Injured	Shooter
Oct 26, 2008	Uni. of Central Arkansas (Arkansas)	2	1	4 unnamed young men
Nov 12, 2008	Dillard High School (Florida)	1	0	Teah Wimberly (15)
Jan 9, 2009	Dunbar High School (Illinois)	0	5	Georgio Dukes (18)
April 26, 2009	Hampton Uni. (Virginia)	0	3	Odane Greg Maye (18)
May 18, 2009	Havard College (Massachuetts)	1	0	Jabrai Copney (20), Jason Aquino (23), Blayn Jiggetts (19)
May 18, 2009	Larose Louisiana	1 (shooter)	0	Justin Doucet
June 16, 2009	International Studies Academy (California)	0	3	unnamed shooter
Sept. 3, 2009	Skyline College (California	0	1	Germaine B. Benjamin (18), Dimaryea J McGhee (20)& Jacori W Bender (18)
Feb 5, 2010	Discovery Middle School (Alabama)	1	0	Hammad Memon (14)
Feb 12,2010	Uni. Of Alabama (Alabama)	3	3	Prof. Amy Bishop (44)
Feb 19,2010	Northern Illinois Uni. DeKalb (Illinois)	0	1	Zachary R. Issacman (22)
Feb 23, 2010	Deer Creek Middle School (Colorado)	0	2	Bruco Strong Eagle Eastwood (32)
March 9, 2010	Ohio State University (Ohio)	2 including shooter)	1	Nathaniel Brown
May11, 2010	West Bladen High School (N Carolina)	0	1	unnamed shooter
Sept 8, 2010	Mumford High School (Michigan)	0	2	Steven Jamal Hare (15)

Date	Location	Fatalities	Wounded	Shooter
Sept 28. 2010	University of Texas (Texas)	1 (shooter)	1	Colton Tooley (19)
Oct 1, 2010	Alisal High School	1	0	unnamed shooter
Oct 8, 2010	Kelly Elementary School Playground (California)	0	2	Brendan O'Rouke
Date	**Location**	**Fatalities**	**Wounded**	**Shooter**
Nov29, 2010	Marinette High School (Wisconsin)	1 (shooter)	0	Samuel Hengel (15)
Dec 6, 2010	Aurora Central High School (Colorado)	0	1	Luis Enrique-Guzman Rincon (20)
Jan 5, 2011	Millard Smith High School (Nebraska)	2 (Including shooter)	2	Robert Butler Jr. (18)
March 25, 2011	MartinsvilleWest Middle School (Indiana)	0	1	Michael Phelps (15)
March 31, 2011	Worthing High School (Texas)	1	5	multiple gunmen
	Highlands Intermediate School (Hawaii)			Male student (14) & 2 more - unnamed
Aug 19, 2011	Albany State University (Georgia)	0	1	unnamed
Oct 24, 2011	Cape Fear High School (N Carolina)	0	1	Charles Underwood (15)
Dec8, 2011	Radford University (Virginia)	2 (including shooter)	0	Ross Truett-Ashley (22)
Dec 9, 2011	Harvard Middle School, Edinburgh (Texas)	0	2	accidental ?
Jan 10, 2012	North Forest High School (Texas)	0	1	18 year old unnamed student
Feb 27, 2012	Chardon High School (Ohio)	3	3	Thomas "T.J." Lane (17)

Date	Location	Fatalities	wounded	Shooter
March 6, 2012	Episcopal School of Jacksonville (Florida)	2 (Including shooter)	0	Shane Schumerth
April 2, 2012	Oikos University (California)	7	3	One L Goh (43)
Aug 16, 2012	Hamilton High School (Tennessee)	0	2	unknown
Aug 27, 2012	Perry Hall School (Maryland)	0	1	Robert Gladden (15)
Sept 7, 2012	Normal Community High School	0	0	unnamed student aged 14
Oct 19, 2012	Banner Academy South (Illinois)	1	0	5 unnamed attackers
Oct 31, 2012	University of Southern California (California)	0	4	Brandon Spencer (20)
Dec 14, 2012	Sandy Hook Elementary School (Connecticut)	28 Including shooter)	2	Adam Lanza (20) First killed his mother, then young children teachers, principal., psychologist & himself
Date	**Location**	**Fatalities**	**wounded**	**Shooter**
Jan 10, 2013	Taft Union High School (California)	0	2	Bryan Oliver (16)
Jan 12, 2013	Osborn High School (Michigan)	0	1	unnamed 16 year old student
Jan 15, 2013	Stevens Institute of Business & Art(Missouri)	0	2	Sean Johnson (34)
Jan 15, 2013	Hazard Community & Technical College (Kentucky)	3	0	Dalton Lee Stidham (12)
Jan 16, 2013	Chicago State University (Illinois)	1	0	Michael McNabb (33) & Brian Hewlett (30)

Date	Location	Killed	Injured	Perpetrator
Jan 22, 2013	Lone Star College-North Harris (Texas)	0	3	unnamed
Jan 31, 2013	Cesar Chavez High School (Arizona)	0	0	rival factions
Jan 31, 2013	Price Middle School	0	2	unnamed 15 year old student
March 18, 2013	University of Central Florida (Florida)	1 The shooter	0	James Oliver Seevakumaran (30)
April 12, 2013	New River Community College (Virginia)	0	2	Neil Allen MacInnis (18)
April 16, 2013	Grambling State University	0	3	unknown assailant
April 18, 2013	Massachusetts Institute of Technology (Massachusetts)	1	0	Brothers Dzhokhar Tsarnaev & Tamerlan Tsarnaev (Boston Marathon bombers)
May 14, 2013	Ossie Ware Mitchell Middle School (Alabama)	0	0	mother of a student (unnamed)
June 7, 2013	Santa Monica (California) including at Santa Monica College	6 including shooter	4	John Zawahri (23) shot father, brother
August 20, 2013	Ronald E McNair Discovery Learning Academy	0	0	Michael Brandon Hill (20)Aug 23, 2013
Aug 23, 2013	North Panola High School (Mississippi)	1	2	gang related 3 men were charged
Aug 30, 2013	Carver High School (N Carolina)	0	1	male student (18)
Oct 4, 2013	Agape Christian Academy (Florida)	0	2	unknown shooter

Date	Location	Fatalities	Wounded	Shooter
Oct 21, 2013	Sparks Middle School (Nevada)	2 including shooter	2	Jose Reyes (12)
Nov 2, 2013	North Carolina A&T State University	0	1	unknown perpetrator
Nov 3, 2013	Stephenson High School (Georgia)	0	2	football team members
Nov 13, 2013	Brashear High School (Pennsylvania)	0	3	drug related incident unknown perpetrators
Dec 4, 2013	West Orange High School (Florida)	0	1	school boy (17) unnamed
Dec 13, 2013	Arapahoe High School (Colorado)	2 including shooter	0	Karl Pierson (18)
Dec 19, 2013	Edison High School (California)	0	1	4 teens 16,16, 17,16 –gang initiationceremony?
Jan 9 2014	Liberty Technology Magnet High School (Tennessee)	0	1	student (16 –unnamed)
Jan 13, 2014	Hillhouse High School (Connecticut)	0	1	unknown perpetrator
Jan 14, 2014	Berrendo Middle School (New Mexico)	0	3	Mason Campbell (12) – suspected shooter – was armed
Jan 17, 2014	Delaware Valley Charter School (Pennsylvania)	0	2	Raisheem Rochwell (17)
Jan 20, 2014	Widener University (Pennsylvania)	0	1	unnamed suspect
Jan 21, 2014	Purdue University (Indiana)	1	0	Cody Cousins(24)
Jan 24, 2014	South Carolina State University	1	0	student (19) unnamed

Date	Location	Fatalities	Wounded	Shooter
Jan 25, 2014	Los Angeles Valley College (California)	1	0	2 men apprehended
Jan 27, 2014	Rebound High School (Illinois)	0	1	student (18) charged
Jan 28, 2014	Tennessee State University	0	1	
Jan 30, 2014	Eastern Florida State College (Florida)	0	1	3 students - all claimed self-defense
Jan 31, 2014	North High School (Iowa)0	0	1	
Feb 10, 2014	Salisbury High School (North Carolina)	0	1	student (17) charged
Feb 10, 2014	Charles F Brush High School	0	0	
Date	**Location**	**Fatalities**	**Wounded**	**Shooter**
Feb 12, 2014	University of Southern California	0	1	
Feb 22, 2014	Georgia Regents University (Georgia)	0	1	policeman &a male suspect involved
March 25, 2014	Benjamin Banneker High school (Georgia)	0	0	multiple people involved
April 11, 2014	East English Village Preparatory Academy (Michigan)	1	0	?
May 4, 2014	Paine College (Georgia)	0	1	2 suspects not of the college
May 5, 2014	Paine College (Georgia	0	1	2nd incident in 2 days, Suspect apprehended
May 8, 2014	Georgia Gwinnett College	0	1	?

Date	Location	Killed	Injured	Notes
May 23, 2014	Isla Vista School	6	13	Rodger, white male
May 14. 2014	John F Kennedy High School (California)	0	1	suspect at large
June 5, 2014	Seattle Pacific University	1	3	Aaron Rey Ybarra (26) charged with premeditated & attempted murder
June 10, 2014	Reynold's High School (Oregon)	2 including shooter	1	Jared Padgett (15)
Sept. 9, 2014	School Miami Florida	0	1	Group of students questioned
Sept 11, 2014	Taylorsville, Utah	0	1	accidental shooting
Sept 27. 2014	Indiana State University	0	1	shooter arrested
Sept 30, 2014	Albemarle High School (N Carolina)	0	1	???
Sept 30, 2014	Fern Creek Traditional High School (Kentucky)	0	1	Shooter arrested
Oct 3, 2014	Langston Hughes High School parking lot (Georgia)	1	0	Eric Dana Johnson Jr. turned himself in later
Oct 24, 2014	Marysville Pilchuck High School	5 including the shooter	1	Jaylen Fryberg (15)
Nov 20, 2014	Florida State University (Florida)	1(the shooter)	3	Myron May (alumnus)fatally shot by police
Nov 20, 2014	Miami City Carol School (Florida)	1	1	???
Dec 12, 2014	Rosemary Anderson High School (Oregon)	0	4	2 men 18 & 22 were arrested

Date	Location			Description
Jan10 2015	Umpqua Community College(Oregon)	9	9	male
Jan15, 2015	Wisconsin Lutheran High School	0	3	Man (36) charged
Jan 16, 2015	Ocala, Florida	0	2	???
Feb 4, 2015	Fredrick High School (Maryland)	0	2	No one apprehended
Feb 14, 2015	Tenya Middle school parking lot (California)	1	0	shooting after school hours. No one apprehended
Feb 23, 2015	Bethune Cookman University (Florida)	0	3	No one apprehended
March 30, 2015	Pershing Elementary School (Missouri)	0	1	one arrested
April 13,2015	Wayne Community College (N Carolina)	1	0	Kenneth Stencil (20) an admitted Neo-Nazi was charged
April 16, 2015	Outside J. B. Martin Middle School (Louisiana)	0	1	Police officer shot. Suspect apprehended
April 27, 2015	North Thurston High School (Washington)	0	0	Student (15) was safely disarmed by a teacher – Brady Olson. Facing charges
May 12, 2015	In a school bus (Florida)	0	2	a student (16) shot 5 bullets into the bus
May 24, 2015	Southwestern Classical Academy parking lot (Michigan)	0	7	2 men apprehended & charged
Aug 27, 2015	Savannah State University (Georgia)	1	0	unidentified shooter

Sept 3, 2015	Sacramento City College (California)	1	2	suspect not arrested
Sept 14, 2015	Delta State University (Mississippi)	2 (including shooter)	0	
Sept 30, 2015	Harrisburg High School (South Dakota)	0	1	student (16) arrested & charged
Oct 1, 2015	**Umpqua Community College (Oregon)**	**10 Including shooter**	**9**	Christopher Harper-Mercer(26)
Oct 9, 2015	North Arizona University	1	3	student (18) arrested & charged
Oct 9, 2015	Texas Southern University (Texas)	1	1	unknown shooter
Oct 22, 2015	Tennessee State University (Tennessee)	1	3	No one arrested or charged

Date	Location	Fatalities	Wounded	Shooter
Nov 1, 2015	Winston Salem State University (North Carolina)	1	1	unknown suspect not apprehended
Nov 20, 2015	Mojave High School (Nevada	1	0	many people involved
Jan 22, 2016	Lawrence Central High School	0	1	Unknown shooter
Jan 29, 2015	Franklin High School (Pennsylvania)	0	0	3 people detained
Feb 9, 2016	Muskegon Heights High School (Michigan)	0	4	No one apprehended
Feb 12, 2016	Independence High School (Arizona)	2 (including shooter)	0	2 girls (15) – apparent murder-suicide
Feb 29, 2016	Madison High School (Ohio)	0	4	James Austin-Hancock (14) Apprehended

Date	Location	Fatalities	Wounded	Shooter
April 23, 2016	Antigo High School (Wisconsin)	1(the shooter)	2	Jakob Wagner (18) died in hospital
June 1, 2016	UCLA (California)	3 including shooter	0	Mainak Sarkar (38) Killed himself
June 8, 2016	Jeremiah Burke High School (Massachusetts)	1	3	2 suspects arrested
Sept 9, 2016	Alpine High School (Texas)	1 (shooter)	2	female student (14) later committed suicide
Sept 28, 2016	Townwille Elementary School (South Carolina)	2	2	student (teenager) also killed father.
Oct 11, 2016	Vigor High School (Alabama)	0	1	student (16) charged
Oct 13, 2016	Linden McKinley STEM Academy (Ohio)	0	2	shooter unknown
Oct 18, 2016	June Jordan High School for Equity (California)	0	4	2 people arrested
Oct 25, 2016	Union Middle School (Utah)	0	1	shoot-out b/w 2 students (14 & 16 years)
Dec 1, 2016	Mueller Park Junior High School (Utah)	0	0	student (15) arrested
Jan 20 2017	West Liberty Salem High School	0	1	student (17) arrested
Jan 20 2017	Red Square at University of Washington (Washington)	0	1	Shooter turned himself in. Was released w/o charges
Date	**Location**	**Fatalities**	**Wounded**	**Shooter**
Jan 27, 2017	Indian Prairie School District 204 (Illinois)	1	0	unknown shooter

March 21, 2017	King City High School	0	1	A suspect arrested in Aug 2017
April 10, 2017	North Park Elementary School (California)	3 (including shooter)	1 injured by bullet	Cedric Anderson (53) shot wife a student then committed suicide
May 4, 2017	North Lake College (Texas)	2 Including shooter	0	Adrian Victor Torres later committed suicide
Sept 13, 2017	Freeman High School (Washington)	1	3	Caleb Sharpe (15) later shot himself taken into police custody
Sept 20, 2017	Mattoon High School (Illinois)	0	1	male student (14) taken into police custody
Nov 13, 2017	Albany State University (Georgia)	0	2	
Nov 14, 2017	Rancho Tehama Reserve (California)	6 including shooter	18	Kevin Neal (43)
Dec 7, 2017	Aztec High School	3 including shooter	0	William Atchison (21) Suicide
Jan 10, 2018	Denison Texas	0	0	A student found a gun & fired it not knowing it was loaded
Jan 20, 2018	Wake Forest University (North Carolina)	1	0	Shot at a party
Jan 22, 2018	Italy High School (Texas)	0	1	Male student (16) shot ex girlfriend (15). Arrested

Date	Location	Fatalities	Wounded	Shooter
Jan 22, 2018	Net Charter High School parking (Louisiana)	0	1	person arrested
Jan 23, 2018	Marshall County High School (Kentucky)	2	18	Gabriel Ross parker (15)
Jan 25, 2018	Mobile Alabama	0	0	Jonah Neal (16) Was arrested & charged. School Incident
Date	**Location**	**Fatalities**	**Wounded**	**Shooter**
Jan31, 2018	school parking lot Philadelphia, (PA)	1	0	Police looking for male suspect
Feb 1, 2018	Sal Castro Middle School (California)	0	5	girl (12) arrested
Feb 5, 2018	Oxon Hall High School (Maryland)	0	1	2 students arrested & charged
Feb 9, 2018	Pearl Cohn High School (Tennessee)	0	1	
Feb 14, 2018	Northern IllinoisUni	5	21	Black Male
Feb 14, 2018	**Marjory Stoneman Douglas High School (Parkland Florida)**	17	17	Nikolas Cruz (19) Activated the fire-alarm ; shot students & staff walked away to a MacDonald's where he was arrested
Feb 24, 2018	Savannah State University (Georgia)	1	0	victim died later
Feb 27, 2018	Missisippi Valley State University	0	1	injury not life-threatening
Feb 27, 2018	Norfolk State University ((Virginia)	0	1	injury not serious

Date	Location	Fatalities	Wounded	Shooter
March 2, 2018	Central Michigan University	2	0	Eric Davies Jr. (19) shot his parents when they came to campus. Then he fled. Police arrested him 15 hrs later & charged him.
March 7, 2018	Huffman High School (Alabama)	1	2	male student (17)
March 7, 2018	Jackson State University (Mississippi)	0	1	injuries not life-threatening
March 8, 2018	University of South Alabama	0	1	I hospitalized after being shot
March 9, 2018	Fredrick Douglas High School	0	1 (Shooter)	Male (16) shot himself accidentally in class. Charged
March 13, 2018	Seaside High School (California)	0	1	Teacher accidentally discharged fire arm injuring 1 student
March 14, 2018	University of Alabama	2 including shooter	1 disgruntled employee shot 2 hospital staff killing one and himself	
Date	**Location**	**Fatalities**	**Wounded**	**Shooter**
March 20, 2018	Great Mills High School (Maryland)	2 including shooter	1	male student (17)
April 12, 2018	South Middle School (Missouri)	0	1	

Date	School	Killed	Injured	Notes
April 20, 2018	Forest High School (Florida)	0	1	Student (19) shot through door as others prepared to go out for gun control. Had planned on more serious damage. Was charged
May 11, 2018	Highland High School (California)	0	1	Shooter (14) shot & injured a student (15) then ditched the gun. Arrested & charged
May 16, 2018	Dixon High School (Illinois)	0	1(shooter)	student (19) Shot by resource officer
May 18, 2018	**Santa Fe High School (Texas)**	**10**	**13 Including shooter**	Dimitrios Pagourtzis had a few guns& other home-made bombs
May 18, 2018	Mount Zion High School (Georgia)	1	3	argument led to shooting in the parking lot
May 25, 2018	Noblesville West Middle School (Indiana)	0	2	unnamed shooter. Shot female student & science teacher Jason Seamen
Aug 17, 2018	Palm Beach Central High School (Florida)	0	2	
Aug 20, 2018	Georgia State University	0	0	shooter unnamed
Aug 30, 2018	Balboa High School (San Francisco, Calif)	0	1	student jokingly discharged gun. $ students arrested

Date	Location	Fatalities	Wounded	Shooter
Sept 5, 2018	Central High School (Rhode Island)	1	1 the Shooter	Student (16)
Sept 10, 2018	Fairley High School (Tennessee)	0	1	unnamed shooter fired into the school bus
Date	**Location**	**Fatalities**	**Wounded**	**Shooter**
Sept 11, 2018	Canyon Springs High School (Nevada)	1	0	unnamed shooter
Oct 29, 2018	David W Butler High School (North Carolina)	1	1	Jatwan Craig Cuffie (16) arrested & charged
Dec 13, 2018	Dennis Intermediate School (Indiana)	1 (Shooter)	0	Mother informed police of his intentions still he shot at officers & when cornered shot himself
Jan 25, 2019	Mobile Alabama	0	2	Student (15) fled the scene. Was caught 24 hrs later – 1st case
Jan 31, 2019	Manassas High School Memphis	0	1	unnamed shooter
Feb 8, 2019	Fredrick Douglas High School (Maryland)	0	1	man (25)shot & injured the school staff member
Feb 12, 2019	Kansas City Missouri	1	0	unnamed shooter
Feb 14, 2019	V. Sue Cleveland High School (New Mexico)	0	0	student (16) Joshua Cleveland
Feb 17, 2019	Eagle Crest High School Parking lot	1	0	2 men I shot the other

Date	Location	Killed	Injured	Notes
Feb.26, 2019	Robert E. Lee High School	0	1	a17 yrs. student had shot another shot another student before this one
Feb. 28, 2019	Cheyenne South High School	0	0	17 yrs student fired at an unoccupied car window in the school parking
March7, 2019	Grambling State Uni.	0	1	accidental firearm discharge by a student
March 22, 2019	Blountville Elementary School (Alabama)	0	1	Substitute teacher
March 27, 2019	Holmes County Mississippi	0	1	either student fired from a bus at another or a drive by shooting
April 1, 2019	Prescott High School (Arkansas)	0	1	male student (14) apprehended
April 25, 2019	Wynbrooke Elementary School	0	10	14 yr. old shot & wounded10 kids
April 25, 2019	College of the Mainland, Texas	0	3	21 yr. old Clayton Whately discharged gun accidentally cadet
April 30, 2019	Uni. of North Carolina, Charlotte Campus	2	4	a shooter
May 4, 2019	Lane Community College	1	0	a 21 yr. old killed on Uni. Of Oregon campus
May 6, 2019				

| May 7, 2019 | Colorado STEM school (science technology, engineering & math) | 1 | 7 | 2 students - Devon Erickson 18 & Maya Mckinney, 16 (|
| May 7, 2019 | Savannah State University | 0 | 1 | man – not student of Uni. |

year	fatalities	wounded	total	comment
1985	7	41	48	all teenagers
1986	**4**	**79**	**83**	**Wyoming school adult shooters**
1987	5	3	8	1 shooter was12 yrs old
1988	10	21	31	mostly young except 1
1989	7	33	40	All teens
1990	0	3	3	all teens; race related
1991	9	1	10	all teens, 1was 24yrs old
1992	11	37	48	mostly young men
1993	9	5	14	young men
year	fatalities	wounded	total	comments
1994	8	9	17	mostly teens
1995	5	5	10	all teens
1996	15	7	22	mostly teens
1997	9	17	26	all teens
1998	**13**	**(Oregon 25) 43**	56	all young teens
Date	Fatalities	Wounded	Total	comments
1999	**(Columbine15) 19**	**(Columbine 21) 33**	52	Columbine killing all teens
2000	6	3	9	I a **6 yr old child** 3 were 13 yrs old 2 were adults

2001	5	19	24	mostly teens
2002	9	9	18	teens & adults
2003	6	5	11	mostly teens & 1 adult
2004	1	5	6	mostly teens
2005	(Minnesota 10) 12	11	23	all teens
2006	15	20	35	teens & adults
2007	**(Virginia 33)** 36	**(Virginia 23)** 30	66	teens
2008	17	30	47	teens & young adults
2009	2	12	14	18-20 yrs olds
2010	9	14	23	teens & adults
2011	5	12	17	teens & I young adult
2012	**(Sandy Hook 28)** 41	**2** 18	30 59	20 kids 6 to 7years 6 adults mum &self all teens
2013	17	34	51	**26 shootings** Mostly teens
2014	21	50	71	**35 shootings** Mostly teens

year	fatalities	wounded	total	**comments**
2015	(Umpqua 10) 30	(Umpqua 9) 51	81	**(24 shootings)**
2016	9	25	34	mostly teens
2017	16	29	45	(California shooting) mostly teens
2018	59	Parkland 1 131	**(Kentucky 18)** **(Illinois 21)** **(Parkland 17)** 190	
until end of May 2019	4	23	27	**40 shootings** mostly teens

Shootings increased in frequency from 2013 and peaked in 2018.

It is a wrong trend that so many shootings take place at schools. Children and young people should not be allowed access to guns as they are not mature enough to handle them with care. Guns are weapons that should never be allowed in the vicinity of any educational institution.

Another thing that became obvious while researching this is that most of the killings were committed by young people. So Again I state young people should not be allowed access to guns. They have no control over their emotions and educational institutions are meant for gaining knowledge not for getting killed. Teachers should pay more attention to at risk students and make psychological treatment easily available to them. Prevention of such crimes is obligatory. It is a blot on us that such things happen on our watch.

Shooting & Massacre AU

Date	Location	Fatalities	Wounded	Comments
Aug 30,1990	Surry Hills New South Wales(NSW)	5	7	Paul Anthony – surrenderedtopolice (shotgun)
Aug 17, 1991	Strathfield NSW Murder-suicide	7	6	Wade Frankum – spree shooting
Oct 27, 1992	Terrigal (Central Coast) NSW	6	1	Malcolm George Baker – spree shooting
Feb 21, 1993	Greenrough Western Australia (WA)	4	0	William Patrick Mitchell (BillMitchell) axed Karen MacKenzie & 3 kids
March 1993	Cangai NSW	5	0	Leonard Leadbeater, Robert Steele & Raymond Basset Went on a 9-day rampage. Took 4 kids hostages in Hanging Rock. Left them unharmed but killed 5 others
Jan 25, 1996	Hillcrest, Queensland (QSLD) murder-suicide	6	0	Peter May went on a rampage. Shot dead 6 family members & himself
April 28, 1996	Port Arthur, Tasmania (TAS) The Port Arthur Massacre	35	24	Martin Bryant went on a shooting spree. John Howard's govt. bought back 750.000 guns. Crime went down. Stricter gun laws.

Date	Location	Fatalities	Wounded	Comments
June 28 1997	Richmond TAS murder-suicide	5	0	Peter Shoobridge cut the throats of his 4 sleeping daughters then cut off one of his hands & killed himself with a shotgun
Oct 8, 1999	Adelaide South Australia (SA)	3	2	Hell's Angels gang feud – mass shooting
June 23, 2000	Childers, QSLD Childers Backpackers Hostel Fire	15 5 UK; 2 Welsh, 3 AU 2 Netherlands, 2 Japan, 1 Irish	10	Robert Paul Long, evicted earlier set fire twice in 1 night
Date	**Location**	**Fatalities**	**Wounded**	**Comments**
July 10, 2001	North Ryde NSW	3	0	Sef Gonzales killed parents & sister by bashing, strangling & stabbing them. Then pretended crimes committed by others. Finally arrested June 13, 2002 ; sentenced to 3 life sentences without parole on May 20, 2004
Oct 21, 2002	Melbourne, VIC Monash University Victoria	2	5 including lecturer	Huan Yun "Allen" Xiang
April 22, 2003	Brisbane QSLD Singh Family Murders	3	0	Max Sica Italian boyfriend of Neelma killed her & siblings by strangling & garden fork & spade. Was imprisoned

Date	Location	Fatalities	Wounded	Comment
Sept 15, 2003	Wilberforce, NSW Poulson family murders	4	0	Phitack Kongsom killed Marilyn (4); Sebastian (1) & their grandfather Peter. with a knife Then shot himself
March 20, 2005	Hunter Valley NSW Oakhampton Heights shooting	4	0	Sally Winter shot her 2 children, husband & herself
Sept 4, 2005	Winchelsea VIC	3	0	Robert Donald William Farquharson drove his 3 sons into a farm dam. They drowned. He was charged convicted, retried & reconvicted in 2010
Feb 20, 2006	Annerley, QSLD	3	0	Errol Graham Hayes set fire to his ex lawyer, Theresa Marchetti's home killing their son & her then partner Mark Christensen. He was charged with murder & 2 counts of arson
Date	**Location**	**Fatalities**	**Wounded**	**Comment**
Feb 7, 2009 at its worst under control Feb 19, 2009	Churchill VIC Churchill fires	11		Was not under control till Feb 19. Destroyed 145 homes & 25,861 hectares

July 18, 2009	North Epping NSW Lin Family murders	5		All were bludgeoned to death Kathy, Min Lin's sister discovered the bodies May 5, 2011 Kathy's husband Lian Bin "Robert" XIE was arrested & charged
April 29, 2011	Hectorville SA (South Australia)	3	3	Arthur Carbo killed 3 and wounded 3 including 2 police officers
Nov 18, 2011	Sydney NSW Quaker Hill nursing home fire	14		Roger Dean, a nurse dependent on drugs committed arson & was jailed for life
Sept 4, 2014	Rozelle NSW	3	2	Adeel Ahmad Khan killed Chris Noble. Bianka O'Brienand her son Jude. He was jailed for 30 years on manslaughter charges.
Sept 9, 2014	Lockhart NSW Hunt family murders	5	0	Geoff Hunt killed his wife &3 kids before shooting himself
Oct 23, 2014	Wedderburn, VIC	3	0	Ian Francis Jamieson shot to death Peter, Mary Lockhart & their son Greg Holmes. Family members have asked for stronger gun control laws.

Date	Location	Fatalities	Wounded	Comments
Dec 15-16, 2014	Lindt Chocolate Café, Sydney NSW	3 2 hostages & gunman	1	Haron Monis held hostage 20 customers & 8 employees for 16 hours. Tactical Operations Unit shot Monis dead
Dec 19, 2014	Cairns QSLD Cairns Child Killings	8 kids between 18 months & 15 years	1 self-inflicted by perpetrator	Raina Mersane Ina Thaiday killed 7 of her kids & her niece. She was charged with murder
Oct 17, 2016	Davidson, North Sydney, NSW	4		Fernando Manriqueused CO(Carbon Monoxide gas to kill himself, his wife & 2 kids
Jan 20, 2017	Melbourne, VIC	6	30	Dimitrious Gargasoulas drove a Holden Commodore into Bourke St Mall. He was arrested & Charged
March 1, 2017	Footscray, VIC Abandoned warehouse used by squatters	3		Darren Patrick Glover set fire to a disused warehouse killing his former Partner Tanya, her boyfriend David & her daughter Zoe who were homeless squatters taking shelter there

May 11, 2018	Osmington, WA	7		A grandfather shot his 4 grandchildren, his wife, daughter & himself. A murder-suicide
Date	Location	Fatalities	Wounded	Comments
July 15, 2018	Ellenbrook, WA	3	0	Teancum Vernon Petersen-Crofts (19) allegedly murdered his mother, sister and brother. He was arrested & sent to the secure Frankland Centre Unit at Graylands
Sept 3, 2018	Bedford, WA	5	0	Anthony Harvey murdered his wife & their 3 children then went to work, mowing lawns for Jim's Mowing. The next day he murdered his mother-in-law. He used a blunt instrument & knives. He was arrested.

Year	No. of murders	Fatalities	Wounded	Comments
1990	1	5	7	Shotgun
1991	1	7	6	Gun
1992	1	6	1	Gun
1993	1	5	0	Axe
1996	**2**	**6** **35**	**0** **24**	**Gun** **Port Arthur Massacre - Gun**
1997	1	5	0	Knife & gun
1999	1	3	2	Gun
2000	1	15	unknown	Arson

2001	1	3		Bashing, strangling &stabbing
2002	1	2	5	Gun
2003	2	3 4		Strangling &Garden fork & spade Knife & gun
2005	2	4 3		Gun car (drowning)
2006	1	3		Fire
2009	1	5		Blunt instrument
2011	2	3 11	3	Gun (siege) Arson
2014	5	3 5 3 2 8	2 1(self-inflicted)	Arson Gun Gun & knife Gun Gun
2016	1	4		carbon monoxide gas
2017	2	6 3	30	Vehicle Fire
2018	2	3 5		Blunt instrument & knife stabbing

Children should never be traumatised in this way. It is worse when children do the shooting. It rips apart the fabric of society. It takes away their innocence and being in such a situation it can lead the traumatised children, especially those without strong family ties to devalue life. The time to sit by and do nothing except spout platitudes is over. It is time for us to protect our precious children – no matter what it takes. Children should enjoy these years not start at every shadow and every noise.

Shooting & Massacre Australia

Most of the shootings and massacres in Australia were committed by adults. Shooting was rare. Knife, arson strangling, garden/farm equipment were common, perhaps because they are more readily available. Australia has stricter gun laws than the States.

Date	Location	Fatalities	Wounded	Comments
Aug 30,1990	Surry Hills New South Wales (NSW)	5	7	Paul Anthony –surrendered to police (shotgun)
Aug 17, 1991	Strathfield NSW Murder-suicide	7	6	Wade Frankum – spree shooting
Oct 27, 1992	Terrigal (Central Coast) NSW	6	1	Malcolm George Baker – spree shooting
Feb 21, 1993	Greenrough Western Australia (WA)	4	0	William Patrick Mitchell (Bill Mitchell) axed Karen MacKenzie & 3 kids
March 1993	Cangai NSW	5	0	Leonard Leadbeater, Robert Steele & Raymond Basset Went on a 9-day rampage. Took 4 kids hostages in Hanging Rock. Left them unharmed but killed 5 others
Jan 25, 1996	Hillcrest, Queensland (QSLD) murder-suicide	6	0	Peter May went on a rampage. Shot dead 6 family members & himself

Date	Location	Fatalities	Wounded	Comments
April 28, 1996	**Port Arthur, Tasmania (TAS) The Port Arthur Massacre**	**35**	**24**	**Martin Bryant went on a shooting spree. John Howard's govt. bought back 750.000 guns. Crime went down. Stricter gun laws.**
June 28 1997	Richmond TAS murder-suicide	5	0	Peter Shoobridge cut the throats of his 4 sleeping daughters then cut off one of his hands & killed himself with a shotgun
Oct 8, 1999	Adelaide South Australia (SA)	3	2	Hell's Angels gang feud – mass shooting
June 23, 2000	Childers, QSLD Childers Backpackers Hostel Fire	15 5 UK; 2 Welsh, 3 AU 2 Netherlands, 2 Japan, 1 Irish	10	Robert Paul Long, evicted earlier set fire twice in 1 night
Date	**Location**	**Fatalities**	**Wounded**	**Comments**
July 10, 2001	North Ryde NSW	3	0	Sef Gonzales killed parents & sister by bashing, strangling & stabbing them. Then pretended crimes committed by others. Finally arrested June 13, 2002 ; sentenced to 3 life sentences without parole on May 20, 2004

Oct 21, 2002	Melbourne, VIC Monash University Victoria	2	5 including lecturer	Huan Yun "Allen" Xiang
April 22, 2003	Brisbane QSLD Singh Family Murders	3	0	Max Sica Italian boyfriend of Neelma killed her & siblings by strangling & garden fork & spade. Was imprisoned
Sept 15, 2003	Wilberforce, NSW Poulson family murders	4	0	Phitack Kongsom killed Marilyn (4); Sebastian (1) & their grandfather Peter. with a knife Then shot himself
March 20, 2005	Hunter Valley NSW Oakhampton Heights shooting	4	0	Sally Winter shot her 2 children, husband & herself
Sept 4, 2005	Winchelsea VIC	3	0	Robert Donald William Farquharson drove his 3 sons into a farm dam. They drowned. He was charged convicted, retried & reconvicted in 2010

Date	Location	Fatalities	Wounded	Comment
Feb 20, 2006	Annerley, QSLD	3	0	Errol Graham Hayes set fire to his ex lawyer, Theresa Marchetti's home killing their son & her then partner Mark Christensen. He was charged with murder & 2 counts of arson
Feb 7, 2009 at its worst under control Feb 19, 2009	Churchill VIC Churchill fires	11		Was not under control till Feb 19. Destroyed 145 homes & 25,861 hectares
July 18, 2009	North Epping NSW Lin Family murders	5		All were bludgeoned to death Kathy, Min Lin's sister discovered the bodies May 5, 2011 Kathy's husband Lian Bin "Robert" XIE was arrested & charged
April 29, 2011	Hectorville SA (South Australia)	3	3	Arthur Carbo killed 3 and wounded 3 including 2 police officers
Nov 18, 2011	Sydney NSW Quaker Hill nursing home fire	14		Roger Dean, a nurse dependent on drugs committed arson & was jailed for life

Date	Location	Fatalities	Wounded	Comments
Sept 4, 2014	Rozelle NSW	3	2	Adeel Ahmad Khan killed Chris Noble. Bianka O'Brienand her son Jude. He was jailed for 30 years on manslaughter charges.
Sept 9, 2014	Lockhart NSW Hunt family murders	5	0	Geoff Hunt killed his wife &3 kids before shooting himself
Oct 23, 2014	Wedderburn, VIC	3	0	Ian Francis Jamieson shot to death Peter, Mary Lockhart & their son Greg Holmes. Family members have asked for stronger gun control laws.
Date	**Location**	**Fatalities**	**Wounded**	**Comments**
Dec 15-16, 2014	Lindt Chocolate Café, Sydney NSW	3 2 hostages & gunman	1	Haron Monis held hostage 20 customers & 8 employees for 16 hours. Tactical Operations Unit shot Monis dead
Dec 19, 2014	Cairns QSLD Cairns Child Killings	8 kids between 18 months & 15 years	1 self-inflicted by perpetrator	Raina Mersane Ina Thaiday killed 7 of her kids & her niece. She was charged with murder

Oct 17, 2016	Davidson, North Sydney, NSW	4		Fernando Manriqueused CO(Carbon Monoxide gas to kill himself, his wife & 2 kids
Jan 20, 2017	Melbourne, VIC	6	30	Dimitrious Gargasoulas drove a Holden Commodore into Bourke St Mall. He was arrested & Charged
March 1, 2017	Footscray, VIC Abandoned warehouse used by squatters	3		Darren Patrick Glover set fire to a disused warehouse killing his former Partner Tanya, her boyfriend David & her daughter Zoe who were homeless squatters taking shelter there
May 11, 2018	Osmington, WA	7		A grandfather shot his 4 grandchildren, his wife, daughter & himself. A murder-suicide

Date	Location	Fatalities	Wounded	Comments
July 15, 2018	Ellenbrook, WA	3	0	Teancum Vernon Petersen-Crofts (19) allegedly murdered his mother, sister and brother. He was arrested & sent to the secure Frankland Centre Unit at Graylands
Sept 3, 2018	Bedford, WA	5	0	Anthony Harvey murdered his wife & their 3 children then went to work, mowing lawns for Jim's Mowing. The next day he murdered his mother-in-law. He used a blunt instrument & knives. He was arrested.

The worst killing was The Port Philip Massacre. There are more deaths through arson or other means. On an average there is one murder a year. This shows that gun control and harsher punishment dissuades the perpetrators from repeating their crimes and makes for a safer world.

Murders in New Zealand

New Zealand has very strict gun laws and is a very safe country. The worst shooting was that of March 2019 when an Australian went to New Zealand and in Christchurch – in two mosques situated away from each other, he shot people when they were at their prayers.

Jessica Arden, the Prime Minister of New Zealand instituted very strict gun control laws and like John Howard, earlier, in 1996, the then Prime Minister of Australia bought back the guns.

Date	Location	Fatalities	wounded	Comments
Nov 13/14, 1990	Aramoana, near Dunedin Otago	14	3	The Aramoana farm murderer David Gray went on a rampage shooting all in his way. Was finally shot by the police
May 20, 1992	Paerata, Auckland region	7		The Schlaepfer Family murder Brian Schlaepfer shot his family & himself. Only granddaughter survived by hiding in a cupboard
June 26, 1992	Masterton	7		The Raymond Ratima murders Raymond Ratima used a knife & killed his wife, children including the unborn baby & in-laws. He was convicted to life imprisonment
June 20, 1994	Dunedin	5		The Bain Family murders David Cullen Bain killed his parents & siblings. Convicted on 5 counts of murder On appeal it appears that his father was the killer. He has since been acquitted.

Feb 4, 1995	Hamilton	6		The Empire Hotel Arson Alan Lory set fire to a couch in the hotel. He was released from prison in 2009
Feb 8, 1997	Raurimu	6		The Raurimu Massacre Stephen Anderson had a history of mental illness he killed 6 people including his father. He was committed to indefinite psychiatric care
March 15, 2019	**Christchurch Masjid Al Noor Linwood Masjid**	**50**	**50**	**Brenton Tarrant, an Australian charged with murder. 3 others also arrested with him. He opened fire as the congregation was praying at the first mosque & then went to the second and opened fire there too.**

New Zealand is a very safe country. Gun laws are very strict and after the latest shooting they have become stricter. The government also bought back guns.

Environmental Issues

Binsey Poplars

felled 1879
By Gerald Manley Hopkins

My aspens dear, whose airy cages quelled,
Quelled or quenched in leaves the leaping sun,
All felled, felled, all are felled;
    Of a fresh and following folded rank
      Not spared, not one
      That dandled a sandlled
    Shadow that swam or sank
On meadow and river and wind-wandering
weed-winding
    bank.

O if we but knew what we do
    When we delve or hew----
Hack and rack the growing green!
    Since country is so tender
To touch her being so slender,
That, like this sleek and seeing ball
But a prick will make no eye at all,
Where we, even where we mean
    To mend her we end her,
    When we hew or delve:
After-comers cannot guess the beauty been.
    Ten or twelve, or ten or twelve
      Strokes of havoc unselve
      The sweet especial scene
    Rural scene, a rural scene
    Sweet especial rural scene.

Environmental issues in the 21ST century

> *What would the world be, once bereft*
> *Of wet and of wildness? Let them be left,*
> *O let them be left, wildness and wet;*
> *Long live the weeds and the wildness yet.*
> *Inversnaid* by GM Hopkins

Our earth is hurtling towards its doom due to our misuse and destruction of our planet and its resources. The environment has become a pervasive and global problem and some of us are aware of it but all of us, especially those in power, ought to join in and help to stem this snowballing situation. There are a diverse number of problems that we need to focus on immediately. What we are doing currently is really not enough. Instead of helping we are in fact harming our environment.

Wherever we look, we see pollution in various forms and pollution of all aspects of the earth. Our forests are fast disappearing due to deforestation in order for us to make houses and cultivate the land as more and more people move from crowded urban areas to suburbs. Green areas are being reduced drastically to make way for tall, concrete housing buildings as the population booms. We are living longer due to advances in medicine and so there is an unprecedented increase in population. Waste product is being carelessly dumped everywhere – not just in our waters. There are more and more landfills that contaminate the air and all who breathe that air. Modern warfare with its bombs and depleted uranium contaminate the air as well as the soil and waterways and lead to various cancers for which there is not always a cure. Water is also toxic due to what goes in it. Global warming has begun which is or should be a major concern for us. Humanity is moving towards a monstrous disaster – a conflagration! There is so much more to say. In fact there is a surfeit of environmental issues today in our world.

<u>Air pollution</u>: this is one of the most difficult to control and so pollution of the air can and does led to diseases and death not just of humans but all living things. Contaminated air is becoming more and more prevalent. This is caused by many factors like burning fossil fuels, The coal industry is extremely bad for air pollution. Then there is hydraulic fracturing, smog, polluted tropospheric ozone, volatile organic compounds, CFC's, heavy metals, motor vehicle exhaust, nitrates and plastics, and also various toxins released by industries and factories.

<u>Water pollution</u>, I think is more controllable than air pollution. It is caused by oil spills, acid rain, industry and factory waste, and urban runoffs. In many places drinking water has become hard and even quite impossible to access easily. Desalinization plants are becoming more prevalent. Rubbish dumped into oceans, industry and factory run offs, bombs, mines etc. – all make the water toxic to aquatic creatures as well as land creatures including man.

<u>Soil pollution</u> is much like water pollution though industry waste plays the greatest part. Nutrients from the soil are leached and the quality of the soil deteriorates sharply. Bombs pollute the soil and the food planted in that contaminated soil leads to various types of cancer. When DU (depleted Uranium) is used, it is even worse.

Developed countries are more guilty than Third world countries though now efforts are being made by many (except USA which is the largest contributor to toxins because President Trump does not share the same views and he has reopened coal mines) to contain and if possible reverse it. Air, water and soil pollution take millions of years to recoup.

Major Environmental issues besides the above are:

<u>Global warming</u>: is the result of emissions of greenhouse gas. This leads to melting of icecaps and glaciers, rising temperatures of oceans and seas, unnatural patterns of precipitation like flash floods, excessive snowfall and desertification. It is also leads to more violent and frequent typhoons, hurricanes, tidal waves etc. In short, it further destabilizes the weather.

<u>Overpopulation</u>: Modern medicine and health care has led to people living longer. It is reaching unsustainable proportions because it will lead to lack of food and other resources. In poorer countries, population explosion and drought has already strained their resources and you hear of starvation, of famine and the accompanying diseases due to weakened immune systems. In many such places it has led to intensive agriculture which means more deforestation and more insecticides, pesticides and fertilizers put into the soil which in turn leads to more toxins in the food chain. It also means the land is not left fallow to recover but replanted immediately. This means the soil is poorer and food planted in such soil has less nutrients.

<u>Waste Disposal</u>: Creation and use of plastics has led to a global waste crisis. Nuclear waste disposal has tremendous health hazards associated with it. Plastic, fast food, packaging and cheap electronic wastes threaten the well-being of humans, animals and aquatic creatures – in fact all living creatures. Waste disposal is one of the most urgent current environmental problems. One can easily see this on the TV or on web pages. In many places, locals have come together to deal with this problem (e.g. India). In some places the use of plastics is being limited but we still have a very long way to go. There are rivers (e.g. the Maribyrnong and Yarra rivers in Melbourne) where it is forbidden to swim or fish due to water toxicity.

<u>Climate Change</u>: has only become apparent in the past two decades but seems to be getting worse. There are new strains of viruses, e.g. a flu virus that kills – one such has been apparent in Melbourne, Australia that has killed a few people in 2019, drastic change in seasons, frequent occurrences of hurricanes, floods, forest fires and droughts all over the world.

<u>Deforestation</u>: Forests are necessary for taking in carbon dioxide and releasing oxygen which we need to breathe. They are also necessary for soil maintenance. Due to industrialization, mechanization, and population explosion, more people are moving to suburbs. So, forests are cut down to accommodate that. This in turn affects the air composition and many animals lose their livelihood and shelter (e.g.

the Koala bears). This has led to many species becoming endangered. At present only 30% or less of land has forest.

Biodiversity: Deforestation and hunting land and marine animals for their fur or tusk for sport has led to the loss of bio-diversity which in turn has affected the earth. Each living creature serves a purpose and when that is no more the balance is upset, which skewers the eco-system. Many coral reefs are dying and disappearing. Some attempt is being made to replant corals. The result is not yet available. Coral reefs support a rich marine life.

Acidity of Oceans: This is the direct result of excessive production of carbon dioxide (CO_2). Humans produce a lot through breathing. Population explosion is only one reason. Deforestation is another. Less plant life means more carbon dioxide in the atmosphere. This leads to increased ocean acidity which especially affects shellfish and plankton. It is feared the ocean acidity may easily rise to 150% by 2100.

Acid Rain: This occurs due to the toxins and pollutants in the atmosphere. Acid rain is caused as a result of combustion of fossil fuels, volcanic eruptions, or rotting vegetables all of which release sulphur dioxide and nitrogen oxides into the air. Acid rain has a serious negative impact on human health, wildlife species and marine life.

Genetic Engineering: a result of this is increased toxins in the modified food and crops which can and does cause environmental and health problems. It is also toxic for animals. Another side effect is insects may grow resistant to the antibiotics. This was the case in Australia in 2019. The flu vaccine had to be modified to stop the insects from becoming impervious to it. The flu virus was potent enough to cause a few deaths.

Mining: Large areas need to be cleared in order for mining to take place – not just deforestation but areas of vegetation around the forests also need to be cleared in order to construct roads and railway tracks to move the mined product. The earth is scarred. Then certain chemicals are used in mining process that causes large scale environmental pollution. Huge profits are to be made in this way.

President Trump has reopened many mines and supports the mining industry. Many precious stones and minerals are mined that have taken a long time to form. Mining also release large quantities of carbon dioxide (mining process, transportation, waste management) excessive water usage and discharge of polluted water. All this for human greed! Mining is a major problem and an important cause of pollution.

<u>Loss of natural resources</u>: The alarming rate of increase in population is a major factor for the loss of natural resources. Some of these are deforestation for building purposes and industries to support the population, animal extinction due to over-hunting or sport – many species are endangered and many have disappeared (like the Tasmanian Devil from Tasmania – in the wild); water shortage is another major issue. All these are connected to population explosion, human greed and disregard of nature and they all affect our ecosystems.

<u>Nuclear problems</u>: We get nuclear energy by splitting atoms. This energy is used for various purposes like producing electricity. This harms the environment in numerous ways. For example it produces radioactive waste which is harmful to all living creatures. Then there is the problem of storing this. So we have to build nuclear power storage facilities. Then there is the fact that decaying radioactive material releases particles that pollute the atmosphere and negatively affects the health of those that breathe in those emissions. All these affect the environment on many levels and human health. It also leads to many types of cancers.

<u>Synthetic Polymers</u>: this is one of the biggest, current environmental issues. Plastic is used everywhere in our lives and that produces large amounts of plastic waste. Plastic is composed of many harmful toxic substances. Because it is easy to carry and dispose in our fast-paced world we have become addicted to plastic things. For example plastic bags, fast food boxes, straws, laptops hats, glasses and eye wear glasses etc. etc. The accumulation of these because they are not biodegradable, leads to their accumulation in huge quantities. And because they are made from toxic compounds for durability, it is not easy to degrade them.

Plastic compounds often kill plant life and affects humans and wildlife negatively. Its toxic compounds cause illnesses and even cancers. It is everywhere. Trash dumps and landfills are serious problems because of plastic. They are hard to dispose of and when they are degraded, they release toxins that affect the atmosphere, water and soil which in turn affects all living creatures. Many large fish and sea mammals die because they get tangled in plastic nets.

Globalization: Globalization has many positive points but it also has some negative outcomes where the environment is concerned. For one thing it has led to increased consumption of products that impact negatively on ecological cycles. Increased usage of goods leads to a stressed environment like transportation of goods and raw materials which can be toxic as in raw materials for industrial use. It also leads to noise pollution and landscape intrusion. Transportation has led to strained non-renewable sources of energy like gasoline. Air travel also contributes massively to the depletion of the ozone layer and to the increasing of greenhouse gases. Industrial waste, often very toxic, is dumped into our oceans and waterways. This kills fish and underwater organisms and deposits harmful chemicals in the waters. Then there are accidents at sea like that of the British Petroleum leak at sea of 2010 that like other such accidents deposits harmful chemicals.

Depleted Ozone layer: Due to air pollution from various sources including planes and bombs the ozone layer is depleted. When bombs fall the air of that country as well as the soil and waterways become polluted. Depleted ozone layers cause cancer, not only in people but also in animals and marine life especially fish in ponds. I saw a lot of fish with cancer caused by the depleted ozone layer over New Zealand. A lot of people in Australia and New Zealand have different kinds of skin cancers. Some have Melanoma which can cause death. All these are interrelated. When one is out of balance, it affects all the others. In recent years there has been an increase in respiratory problems, Asthma, and cardiac-vascular diseases. In Serbia where I was in 2019, there is, since the bombing of FRY and the extensive use of Depleted Uranium, a lot of lung cancer which often also enters the brain. The survival rate is poor. Our poor planet has been treated very shabbily by us. It is now time to redress that and start taking care of our environment and selfishly we would also be taking care of ourselves.

Climate change

> *And for all this, nature is never spent:*
> *There lives the dearest freshness deep down things;*
> *And though the last lights off the black West went*
> *Oh, morning, at the brow brink eastward, springs –*
> *Because the Holy Ghost over the bent*
> *World broods with warm breast and with ah!*
> *Bright wings.*
>
> *God's Grandeur* By <u>Gerard Manley Hopkins</u>

Global warming refers to surface temperature increases, while climate change includes global warming and everything else that increasing greenhouse gas amounts will affect. Global warming and climate change are not the same, contrary to what many people believe. Climate change is the shifts in the weather that affects our climate, rising average temperatures, extreme weather events and the changing conditions of wildlife populations and their habitat e.g. the melting of polar ice and loss of habitat for polar wildlife.

What causes climate change? How does global warming impact on or cause it? These questions must be answered first if we are to understand global warming.

Climate change is caused by many factors – natural and man-made.

Our lives are greatly dependant on the sun's energy. Nearly half of the light that passes through the atmosphere is absorbed and radiated upward in the form of infrared heat. The greater part (about 90%) of this is absorbed by the greenhouse gases in the atmosphere and then re-emitted back towards the surface which is then warmed to the life-supporting 15% Celsius. If there is not enough warmth, life as we know it, cannot exist. If there is too much then it is too hot and again, life as we know it, cannot exist.

Temperature rise due to climate change may radically damage the global economy and slow growth in the coming decades if nothing is done to slow the pace of warming, according to new research. (Justin Worland 22/10/2015). The current global average temperature is 0.85% higher than in the 19th century. This pattern has been going on since 1850. The temperature has increased 2 degrees Centigrade since pre-industrial times and continues to rise. These days it is clearly apparent that temperatures are rising, leading to the polar caps melting and a whole host of resultant catastrophic occurrences.

This is further strengthened by Marshall Burke, asst. prof. Stanford University who said that their study aimed at *providing an estimate of the benefits of reducing emissions.* He went on to say that this study does not take into consideration the impact climate change will have on the rise of sea levels, increased frequency of and velocity of storms that will negatively affect the economy.

Increasing temperatures caused by climate change will make the water of the oceans expand; the ice in the Antarctic and Greenland to melt which will in turn contribute to rising sea level. Low-lying coastal areas such as the Netherlands and Bangladesh, will be at risk and huge tracts of land will be at danger from flooding. This in turn will result in people leaving their homes and taking refuge in cities that are already overcrowded.

Many crops grown around world will also be affected. For example crops like wheat and rice grow well in high temperatures, while plants such as maize and sugarcane prefer cooler climates. Changes in rainfall patterns will also affect how well plants and crops grow. This may affect the food available in many countries falling below the level to support their population and leading to starvation.

Lack of water could be another effect as drought may affect some regions where water is already scarce (central and east Africa). Some areas will get too much water and some too little.

As climate change takes place, our daily weather and normal temperatures will change, the homes of plants and animals will be affected all over the world. Polar bears and seals are a good example of animals that will be affected by climate change, they will have to find new land for hunting and living, if the ice in the Arctic melts, but the fact is more real that these species could become extinct. Climate change has and will have far-reaching consequences on our planet.

Greenhouse gas; (GHG) is a gas that absorbs and emits radiant energy within the thermal infrared range. Greenhouse gases cause the greenhouse effect. The primary greenhouse gases in the Earth's atmosphere are water vapor, carbon dioxide, methane, nitrous oxide and ozone. Without greenhouse gases, the average temperature of Earth's surface would be about −18 °C (0 °F), rather than the present average of 15 °C (59 °F). The atmospheres of Venus, Mars and Titan also contain greenhouse gases.

- Some characteristics of greenhouse gases are:

    Nitrous oxide (N_2O): a powerful greenhouse gas produced through soil cultivation, especially through the use of commercial and organic fertilizers, fossil fuel combustion, nitric acid production and biomass burning.

    Water vapour (H_2O): Most abundant of all the greenhouse gases. Water vapour increases as the earth's surface warms. It also causes clouds to form and precipitation to take place and in this way carries out the greenhouse effect.

    Carbon dioxide, (CO_2): is a vitally important but minor atmospheric component. When oxygen is taken in, carbon dioxide comes out – process of breathing; through volcanic eruptions and in recent centuries through deforestation, land overuse, and burning of fossil fuels especially since the Industrial Revolution

This acts adversely on the atmosphere.

Chlorofluorocarbons (**CFC**s): These are synthetic compounds entirely of industrial origin. When released into the atmosphere, they destroy the ozone layer. They are greenhouse gases.

Methane: This is a hydrocarbon gas found naturally in the atmosphere and also produced by man through activities like agriculture, particularly rice cultivation decomposition of wastes, ruminant digestion and manure management. This is less abundant in the atmosphere than carbon dioxide but a far more active greenhouse gas.

Climate change is caused by nature as well as caused by man.

Nature

Orbital Changes: As the earth rotates and revolves around the sun (at an angle) different areas are exposed to heat and cold which in turn reflects the changes in temperature. This process goes on over tens or hundreds of thousands of years. This has minimal effect on global warming.

Volcanic Eruptions: Such eruptions discharge carbon dioxide but may also discharge aerosols such as volcanic ash or dust, and sulphur dioxide **SO$_2$**. They may also have soot, salt crystals, bacteria and viruses. Aerosols also disperse the incoming solar radiation and thus reduce heat. They may also block out sunlight and cause cooling that may last up to two years. Volcanoes that erupt at lower latitudes are more likely to cause hemispheric or global cooling than volcanoes near the poles, which are more likely to cause cooling because of the sulphurous aerosols which are confined to wind patterns surrounding the poles.

Solar Radiation: Solar radiation varies a little. The change is due to the number of sunspots present. But every 11 years the number of sunspots changes from a maximum to a minimum. The sun emits more radiation during active periods. Because sunspots supress the heat, it flows to the surrounding areas and there is more heat. More sunspots means warmer global climate whereas less sunspots mean it is cooler. About 300 years ago one such period happened and it was called the Little Ice Age.

Movement of the Earth's plates: The tectonic plates move and in due course of time landmasses are moved to different positions. This affects global circulation of air and ocean water and the climate of continents. One example of this effect on the climate is the location of coal mines – mostly in tropical areas. Since the Industrial Revolution, the Northern Hemisphere has warmed more than the Southern hemisphere because ratio-wise the northern hemisphere has a greater land mass in comparison with the water surrounding it.

El Niño- Southern Oscillation (ENSO): Every 3-4 years, El Niño starts over the Pacific Ocean when the trade winds from the East start to weaken. The surface of the water of the Eastern Pacific heats up while the surface of the Western Pacific cools down. Sometimes it is the opposite and then it is known as La Niño. Both affect the circulation patterns of the atmosphere and influence the climate.

Melting Permafrost: Frozen soil has trapped environmental gases for centuries. This is the permafrost. Siberia has one of the largest areas of permafrost in the world. Large tracts are also present in Alaska and Canada. When it melts it releases trapped gases into the air, raises sea levels, narrows habitat like those of the polar animals and food source for polar bears and other polar animals.

Water Vapour: this is simply water in a gaseous form, present in the atmosphere and affecting both climate and weather. As it gets hotter, more water evaporates and later becomes vapour which is also a type of greenhouse gas.

Man Made

We are burning fossil fuels at an unprecedented rate, thus releasing chemicals and foreign substances into the air. These in turn absorb more solar energy which results in global warming and climate change.

Greenhouse Gas Emission: This is the biggest and most prevalent man-made climate enforcer. Greenhouse gas that exists in the atmosphere absorbs the sun's heat and facilitates life. Man, however, produces too large an amount of greenhouse gas so that it upsets the atmosphere's energy balance.

Some of these gases like carbon dioxide and nitrous oxide are long-lived. Methane and some other gases on the other hand, are short lived. But they are produced in huge quantities continually and are thus very potent. All these affect the climate negatively and lead to atmospheric imbalance.

Grime: This is the grime that covers urban buildings. A recent study shows that grime traps and holds nitrous oxide. In hot sun concentrated amounts are released into the air.

Fossil fuels: We burn a lot of fossil fuel. Among other chemicals, it releases a lot of carbon dioxide, which is a major greenhouse gas enforcer and is very long-lived – as much as 50,000 years. In small quantities and on its own it is not dangerous but we produce huge amounts and in conjunction with other greenhouse gases it is causes global warming. This too, is a by-product of burning fossil fuels, biofuels and biomass. When combustion of these is incomplete, they produce soot which enters the atmosphere.

Trump promised to eliminate the Climate Action Plan and allow more drilling on federal land for shale oil and natural gas - fossil fuels. Shale oil prices had fallen to a low since 2014. In time prices rebounded but now with Trump's decision, prices will fall again as supply will be more abundant. This will worsen climate change.

Black Carbon: This is another by-product of fossil fuel. When fossil fuel, biofuel and biomass do not burn properly, they produce soot which enters the air as aerosols (fine particles). These absorb large amounts of heat and infrared radiation. Diesel vehicles even more than other vehicles, release carbon dioxide as also do wildfires, and industrial and residential heating, into the atmosphere.

Deforestation: This removal of forests is bad because forests filter the carbon dioxide and nitrous oxide. They stabilize the environment. So deforestation negatively impacts the environment. Deforestation also affects the soil because tree roots anchor the soil and protect it from being washed away or dispersed due to wind and other weather factors.

Agriculture: Farming produces methane gas and carbon dioxide. With farms getting larger and deforestation going on apace, there is no filter for these chemical which then go into the atmosphere and in due course lead to global warming

Overpopulation As population increases so does the carbon dioxide (through breathing), which is a major and primary greenhouse gas responsible for global warming

Fossil Fuel Drilling All drilling for any kind of fossil fuel releases gases into the atmosphere where a pollution source is created that cannot easily **be neutralised**. This will become worse with the fracking method of fuel extraction.

Agricultural Fertilizers: Fertilizers are needed to grow crops in large quantities to feed the growing population. (Still there is hunger and starvation in the world!) These fertilizers use a form of nitrous oxide which is harmful to the environment because the sun warms and releases the gas which is often taken far from the production areas by waterways or winds.

Power Plants: 44% of all global warming is from emissions from power plants. These emissions are very harmful. The size and concentration of these emissions are too big for the local environment to neutralize and so it is pushed upwards into the atmosphere where it can pollute the whole world – and not only its initial source.

Landfills and Garbage Deposits: These contribute greatly to global warming. The heaps of garbage as they get broken down in the landfills release toxins – nitrous oxide and other environmentally unfriendly gases and huge amounts of heat.

Transportation: All transports use fossil fuel. This is the second largest contributor to global warming. Switching to electric cars is not a real solution as they too, are powered by fossil fuel.

All these in turn impact on global warming. In short climate change is the **complex shifts now affecting our planet's weather and climate systems. Climate change encompasses not only rising average temperatures but also extreme weather events, shifting wildlife populations and habitats, rising seas, and a range of other impacts. All of these changes are emerging as humans continue to add heat-trapping greenhouse gases to the atmosphere.**

President Trump does not believe in Global Warming. I think this is because he does not understand it. On January 29th 2019 he tweeted:

In the beautiful Midwest, wind chill temperatures are reaching minus 6o degrees, the coldest-ever recorded....What the hell is going on with Global warming? It seems to me he is confusing climate with weather.

Climate is atmospheric reaction over a period of time whereas weather is over a short period of time. The rate of greenhouse emission determines the rate of warming or cooling of the globe. President Trump mixes up the two, I believe.

Climate change affects the earth on many levels: environmental, economic and social.

Some recent cold spells are caused by the polar vortex. Evidence suggests that this vortex is being seen more and more outside the Arctic Circle and this is causing the frigid polar air to escape southwards and this is what is causing the kind of cold weather we are now experiencing.

Trump scoffs at global warming. He has said that he aims to build two sea walls on his golf reserve in Scotland to keep the sea at bay. He believes it is global cooling not global warming that we are currently experiencing. He will not be convinced otherwise. He believes it is NOT man-made and so no action is needed from us. On the other hand, the world's top scientists and environmentalists believe it is man who has contributed greatly to the present state of the planet.

Why do men now not reck his rod?
Generations have trod, have trod, have trod
And all is seared with trade; Bleared, smeared with toil
And wears man's smudge and shares man's smell: the soil
Is bare now, nor foot can feel, being shod.
God's Grandeur by GM Hopkins

Climate change affects:

The Environment: *Climate change is a change in the statistical distribution of weather patterns when that change lasts for an extended period of time. Climate change can be caused by factors such as biotic processes, variations in solar radiation received by Earth, plate tectonics, and volcanic eruptions. (Wikipedia)*

The effects of climate change will be felt in our generation as typhoons, floods, forest fires, earthquakes, volcanic eruptions and droughts as throughout 2017 and more specially 2018 and 2019 have shown us. It was expected to take place later but with the melting of the polar ice caps and, the expansion of the ozone layer, the rise in the water levels etc. one cannot escape the fact that all this is clearly linked to our abuse and misuse of the earth's resources.

IPCC (Intergovernmental Panel on Climate Change) co-chairman Prof. Parry said that though we had expected the impacts to appear in our progeny's lifetimes, it now appears we will see and are seeing the **mild** beginning of it now. And for a second just think – if this is the prelude, how much more intense and damaging will the main effects be? And it is we, who are responsible for this state of affairs. Prof Parry put it very succinctly when he said: *We now have a choice between a future damaged world or a severely damaged world.* The report also stated that Africa and the Arctic, Fiji and other small islands, Asian mega deltas like the Mekong would bear the brunt. We have already seen signs of this in recent months.

A warmer atmosphere – some natural and the majority and most potent ones, are man-made. And the guilt is ours for not taking proper care of our inheritance.

- **Hurricanes**: what are hurricanes? Hurricanes are violent tropical storms, formed in low pressure areas and that take place between the Equator and the Tropic of Cancer to the north or the Equator and the Tropic of Capricorn to the south. They usually form at sea and cause violent waves but when they hit land they destroy buildings and everything else in their path. Due to the wind velocity, they often cause flooding. Hurricanes blow in a spiral and the safest place to be in a hurricane is said to be the centre which is referred to as the eye of the storm. Hurricanes are dangerous and destructive. They are also called typhoons and cyclones depending on the area where they occur.

  2018 saw some of the worst hurricanes in a very long time. Some of them in the USA were:

  o **Florence** that hit North Carolina; **Harvey** that hit the Southern Great Plain of the USA, Houston, Texas. The Gulf Coast; **Irma** that hit The Caribbean; **Maria** that lasted a while hit Puerto Rico; **Nate** hit Central America and the North US Coast, **Florence and Michael** that hit South East USA. These were extremely dangerous and caused serious damage some of which is still felt today. Some other hurricanes that were not quite as dangerous but still caused damage were (in alphabetical order): **Alberto, Beryl, Chris, Debby, Ernesto, Gordon, Helene, Isaac, Joyce, Kirk, Leslie, Nadine, Oscar, Patty, Rafael, Sara, Tony, Valerie and William.**

Following are the strongest ones that caused severe to extremely severe damage around the world month by month followed by a general chart. I have not regarded those that didn't leave much damage behind.

o **Fehi** that hit **New Zealand** and **New Caledonia** causing severe damages; **Berguitta** that hit **Mauritius** and **Réunion,** also very strong; **Agathon (Bolaven)** that struck the **Caroline Islands., Phillipines and Vietnam**; **04** that hit **Christmas Island**, **Ava** that struck **Madagascar** and **Joyce** that hit **Western ;Australia.** (January 2018).

o **Gita** that caused severe damages when it hit **Vanatu, Fiji and Futuna, Samoa, American Samoa, Niue, Tonga, New Caledonia, Queensland** and **New Zealand; Sanba (Basyang) (*very strong*)** hit the **Caroline Islands** and the **Phillipines; Kelvin (very severe)** that hit **Western** and **South Australia** (February 2018)

o **18U (extremely damaging) hit the Northern Territory (Aus); Marcus** (even more destructive) hit the top end of **Kimberely** and **Tanimbar Islands; Josie (very strong)** that struck **Vanatu, Fiji** and **Tonga; Eliakim** that damaged **Madagascar** (All strong and all in March 2018)

o **Keni (very destructive)** that affected **Vanatu, Fiji and Tonga; Fakir** (very strong) that affected **Madagascar, Réunion** and **Mauritius** (April 2018)

o **Alberto** (caused severe damage) hit **Yucatan Peninsula, Cayman Islands, Cuba, Gulf Coast of the USA, Southeastern USA, Midwestern USA, Ontario; Sagar** (very severe) **struck Yemen Horn of Africa; Mekunu** strong hit **Yemen, Oman, Saudi Arabia** (May 2018)

o **Ewiniar** (very damaging) struck **Vietnam, Phillipines, South China, Taiwan, Ryukyu Islands; Prapiroon (Florita)** hit **Japan, Korean Peninsula** (June 2018)

o **Jongdari** (caused severe damage) to **Japan, East China; Maria (Gardo)** (very destructive) hit **Mariana Islands, Ryukyu Islands, Taiwan, East China; Son Tinh (Henry) hit Phillipines, South China, Vietnam, Laos,**

Thailand, Myanmar; <u>Ampil (Inday)</u> struck **Ryukyu, China, Russian Far East;<u>13W (Josie)</u> struck Taiwan, Ryukyu Islands, Phillipines, East China (July 2018)**

o <u>Florence</u> very destructive that hit **West Africa, Cape Verde, Bermuda, Southeastern USA, Mid-Atlantic States, Atlantic Canada;** <u>Rumbia</u> hit **Ryukyu Islands, China, Korean Peninsula, Russian Far East;** <u>Jebi (Maymay)</u> hit **Mariana Islands, Taiwan, Japan, Russian Far East, Arctic;** <u>Bebinca</u> hit **South China, Laos, Vietnam Thailand Myanmar;** <u>24W (Luis</u>) hit **Taiwan, East China;** <u>Yagi (Karding</u>) hit **Phillipines, Taiwan, Ryukyu, China;** <u>Cimaron</u> hit **Hawaii;** <u>Soulik</u> **struck Caroline Islands, Mariana Islands, Northeast China, Japan, Korean Peninsula, Russian Far East, Alaska;** <u>Bob 04</u> hit **East India (August 2018)**

o <u>Mangkhut (Ompong</u>) struck **Marshall Islands, Mariana Islands, Phillipines, Taiwan, Hong Kong, Macau, South China, Vietnam;** <u>Trami (Paeng</u>) hit **Mariana Islands, Taiwan, Japan, Russian Far East, Alaska;**

o <u>Leslie</u> hit **Azores, Bermuda, East Coast of USA, Madeira, Iberian Peninsula, France;** <u>Nineteen-E</u> struck **Baja California Sur, Northwestern Mexico, Southwestern USA, Texas, Oklahoma, Arkansas;** <u>Kong-rey (Queenie)</u> hit **Caroline Islands, Mariana Islands, Japan, Taiwan, South Korea,** <u>Sergio</u> struck **Baja California, Northwestern Mexico, Southwestern USA,** <u>Rosa</u> hit **Baja California, Northwestern Mexico, Southwestern USA;** <u>Gordon</u> struck **Greater Antilles, The Bahamas, Florida, Gulf Coast of USA, Eastern USA, Ontario;** <u>Olivia</u> hit **Hawaii; (September 2018)**

o <u>Michael</u> struck **Central America, Yucatan Peninsula, Cayman Islands, Cuba, Southeastern USA, East Coast of the USA, Atlantic Canada, Iberian Peninsula;** <u>Luban</u> hit **Yemen, Oman; Titli struck Andhra Pradesh,**

East India; <u>Willa</u> hit **Central America, Southwestern Mexico, Texas;** Yutu (Rosita) hit **Caroline Islands, Mariana Islands, Plillipines, South China, Taiwan;** <u>Vicente</u> hit **Honduras, El Salvador, Guatemala, Southwestern Mexico (October 2018)**

o <u>**Gaja**</u> **struck Andaman Islands, South India, Sri Lanka;** <u>T**oraji**</u> hit **Vietnam, Malay Peninsula;** <u>**Owen**</u> hit **Solomon Islands, Papua New Guinea, Queensland, Northern Territories;** <u>**Usagi (Samuel)**</u> hit **Caroline Islands, Phillipines, Vietnam, Cambodia, Laos (November 2018)**

o <u>**35W (Usman)**</u> struck **Palau, Phillipines; Phethai** struck **East India, Northeast India** (December 2018)

Earthquake: a sudden violent shaking of the ground, typically causing great destruction, as a result of movements within the earth's crust or volcanic action. The shaking results in the release of energy in the earth's lithosphere which creates seismic waves. Some earthquakes can be very violent while others can be relatively mild. In recent years there has been greater seismic activity than we have seen for a long time. And not only that, some have been very severe and caused serious damage.

Number of earthquakes worldwide for 2009–2019[1][2]

Magnitude	2009	2010	2011	2012	2013	2014	2015	2016	2017	2018	2019
8.0–9.9	1	1	1	2	2	1	1	0	1	1	1
7.0–7.9	16	21	19	15	17	11	18	16	6	16	7
6.0–6.9	144	151	204	129	125	140	124	128	106	117	74
5.0–5.9	1,896	1,963	2,271	1,412	1,402	1,475	1,413	1,502	1,451	1,675	742
4.0–4.9	6,805	10,164	13,303	10,990	9,795	13,494	13,239	12,771	11,296	12,777	5,580
Total	8,862	12,300	15,798	12,548	11,341	15,121	14,795	14,420	12,860	14,586	6,402

Today July 5, 2019 there has been a 6.4 magnitude earthquake in Southern California, Searles Valley and again on July 7, 2019 in Southern California and also in Sacramento and Las Vegas – the strongest in twenty years. This month has also seen a 7.3 quake in Ambonm Maluku in Indonesia. There has also been a quake of 8.2 in Levuka, Eastern Fiji. There have been many small quakes under 4.0 degrees in magnitude around the world.

By death toll

Rank	Death toll	Magnitude	Location	MMI	Depth (km)	Date
1	18	6.1	Philippines, Luzon	VII (*Very strong*)	20.0	April 22
2	13	5.8	China, Sichuan	VIII (*Severe*)	10.0	June 17

By magnitude

Rank	Magnitude	Death toll	Location	MMI	Date
1	8.0	2	Peru, Loreto	VIII (*Severe*)	May 26
2	7.6	0	Papua New Guinea, East New Britain offshore	VII (*Very strong*)	May 14
3	7.5	1	Ecuador, Pastaza	VII (*Very strong*)	February 22
4	7.3	0	Indonesia offshore, Banda Sea	VI (*Strong*)	June 24
5	7.2	0	New Zealand, Kermadec Islands offshore	VII (*Very strong*)	June 15
6	7.1	0	Papua New Guinea, Morobe	VII (*Very strong*)	May 6
7	7.0	1	Peru, Puno	IV (*Light*)	March 1
	6.4		South California	Strong	July 4
	7.1		South California inc Las Vegas	Very strong	July 7

Drought: It is another natural disaster when precipitation in an area falls below the average. This results in shortages of water supply both surface water and ground water. Droughts can last for months or even years. Droughts have a serious impact on the ecosystem, agriculture of the affected area and the economy of the country. Annual dry seasons in tropical areas significantly increase the chances of drought and the resultant bush fires. They also produce arid biomes, deserts and grasslands. However prolonged periods of drought have very negative consequences as they result in mass migrations of peoples.

Due to the re-occurrence of droughts through the centuries, many plant species have adapted, like the cacti, or plants that survive by burying their seed deep in the soil during drought periods.

- In 2018 and 2019 the **drought** in many places followed a strange pattern as heavy rains and storms came after very dry spells. Places that were severely affected were: South-East USA especially Kentucky and Tennessee, California. Colorado, Northern Great Plain, Florida, North East USA, British Colombia, Canada, Argentina, Bolivia, Australia, Switzerland, Italy, Spain, Portugal, South Europe, Inner Mongolia, China, Iran, Afghanistan, India, Sri Lanka, Cape Town (South Africa), Somalia.
- **Excessive and heavy rainfall**: Midwest and South east USA.-.California, Louisiana, Florida, Bolivia, Australia – Queensland.
- **Typhoon Mangkhut** that hit Philippines, Hong Kong and China. **Tornado** that hit Cuba and Turkey and **intense storm** that hit California.
- **Fire** that devastated large areas of California, Northwest USA and Chile. And affected large areas in Australia
- **Sinkholes** in Iran and the Arctic.
- **Volcanic eruptions** in Indonesia, Japan, Chile and Papua New Guinea.

The cryosphere – the frozen water on the Earth's poles is melting. These include mountain glaciers ice sheets of the Antarctic and Greenland. The number of glaciers has been radically reduced

- This in turn has caused sea-levels to rise faster in recent times
- Some species are severely endangered such as the Adélie penguin in Antarctica
- Many species are moving further to the colder areas like certain species of butterflies, foxes as well as some plants

- Though there is heavier rainfall and snow in certain areas other areas are suffering from severe drought, wildfires, loss of crops and water shortages
- Some living creatures like mosquitoes, ticks, bark beetles and jellyfish are thriving and negatively affecting the environment and human health.

Trump withdrew from the Paris deal in 2017 – to be formalised in 2020 after elections.

Economic: Global warming as a consequence of man-made problems like the extensive use of fossil fuels by some countries economically affects us negatively. Under Trump fossil fuel usage has been reinstituted. Coal mining has also begun again.

Some people in his cabinet in important positions, like Trump, do not believe in global warming or are very much into fossil fuels.

- Coal miners are also an important part of Trump's base
- Many important members, top advisers and appointees are direct transplants from the fossil fuel industry like:
    - **Ryan Zinke** – was the Interior Secretary and kept tight control of information especially concerning environmental issues to be published. He is a fossil fuel lobbyist. He was replaced by another of the same ilk, David Bernhardt, who just prior to his appointment had a meeting with a senior executive of Exxon Mobil and head of the American Petroleum Institute. Zinke is a strong supporter for the oil and gas industry: He strongly defended the Trump administration's decision to shrink Utah's Bears Ears and Grand Staircase-Escalante national monuments by 1.1 million acres (or 85 percent). The *Washington Post* revealed that the uranium mining company Energy Fuels Resources had aggressively lobbied Zinke's deputies and the Trump administration also to shrink Bears Ears. When the White House announced that they were going to loosen environmental regulations and repeal the Obama administration's ban on offshore oil and gas drilling in U.S. coastal waters, Zinke was very much in agreement and he and Trump made plans to make 90 percent of currently available offshore waters open to drilling in the next five years, the *New York Times* reported. Ryan Zinke said in a statement. *"This is a clear difference between energy weakness and*

energy dominance. We are going to become the strongest energy superpower."

This is an abuse of the government's regulatory power.

- o **Rick Perry** – Governor of Texas; formerly Chairman of Exxon gas. In this position, he ignored whenever possible the dwindling water supplies, lack of public parkland, the negative results of oil and gas "fracking" boom in north and South Texas and other environmental issues. *Perry has been particularly hostile to environmental concerns — that is, when he's showing any interest at all* according to **the OBSERVER.**
- o **David Bernhardt**: a former lobbyist is the Deputy Interior Secretary. He has pushed to expand oil and gas drilling. He is expected to follow in the footsteps of Zinke and open federal lands to oil, gas and coal development without restrictions. Some policies that Bernhardt has already rolled back regulation on are: fracking and methane leaks, rescinding regulations and royalties, approving a pipeline through right-of-way, reducing protection for endangered species and expanding areas of offshore drilling.
- o **Wilbur Ross:** is the Secretary for Commerce in the Trump administration and thus the principal voice for business. Before this he was a banker known for restructuring failed companies in coal, steel, telecommunications, foreign investments and textiles. He was also known for buying out failed businesses in leveraged buyouts. During his confirmation hearing he 'forgot' to disclose his financial interest in a Russian company. And then during the government shutdown when 800,000 federal workers were expected to work without pay for 35 days, Ross commented that he could not understand why they

had to go to food banks when they could take out bank loans at lower interest rates. That shows you how much in touch he is with the people. It also shows extreme callousness.

o **Scott Pruitt**–EPA Director from 2017 to 2018. A well-noted climate sceptic; a documented supporter for oil and gas companies. Beginning of January 2019 *defended the trump administration's decision to shrink Utah's Bears Ears and Grand Staircase-Escalante national monuments by 1.1 million acres (85%).* It was later uncovered By the Washington Post that the uranium Company Energy Fuels resources had lobbied quite aggressively for this. Jared Keller editor **Pacific Standard** Jan 5, 2019.

It is believed by most that Bernhardt will follow in Pruitt's footsteps and open federal lands to oil, gas and coal development without reconstruction. *Some policies that he has already enacted are:* rolling back regulations on fracking and methane leaks; rescinding royalties regulations; approving a pipeline across right-of-way; reducing protection for endangered species and expanding areas for offshore drilling. He has long been a mouthpiece for oil and gas companies. In 2014 the New York Times published an 84 page correspondence exchange between him and Oklahoma oil and gas group and Devon energy. He became Oklahoma attorney general in 2011. He has got a lot of money donations from oil and gas companies

o **Rex Tillerson** the Secretary of state in the Trump organisation was also the lead player in deciding US International environmental policy, including the Paris climate Accord from which the US led by Trump and with Rex Tillerson as a chief player withdrew. Like some others in Trump's cabinet, Tillerson too was an ExxonMobil product. Previously he had been the Chief Executive of Exxon Mobil. Unlike Pruitt, Tillerson's utterances were more moderate and nuanced.

The Paris Climate Agreement

On June 1, 2017, Trump announced the U.S. withdrawal from the Paris Climate Agreement. 195 signatories had pledged to cut their greenhouse-gas emissions to 26-28 percent below 2005 levels by 2025. They agreed to ratchet emissions to zero by 2100. They committed $3 billion to the poorer countries who are most likely to suffer damage from rising sea levels and other consequences of climate change.

The goal of the agreement is to keep global warming from getting worse to 2 C above pre-industrial levels. A 2018 study shows that temperatures above that level would pass for example the tipping point, the Arctic tundra would thaw, and would release 45,000 years' worth of trapped greenhouse gases. It would create catastrophic warming of 5 degrees Celsius or more. Melting glaciers would increase sea levels by 200 feet.

The United States is responsible for 20 percent of the world's greenhouse gas emissions. The other signatories can't reach the accord's goal without U.S. participation.

Trump said he wanted to negotiate a better deal, but leaders from Germany, France, and Italy said the accord is non-negotiable. China and India joined the other leaders in stating they remain committed to the agreement. Some have argued that America's withdrawal from a leadership position creates a vacuum that China will readily fill.

Business leaders from Tesla, General Electric, and Goldman Sachs said Trump's action would give foreign competitors an edge in clean energy industries. U.S. companies will lose government support and subsidies in these industries.

It will take four years to withdraw formally, making it an issue in the 2020 presidential election.

To conclude this section

The earth is ours to look after it. We are the caretakers. The earth is not here for us to abuse and destroy to misuse and rape.

The world is in serious turmoil and disarray. Even Nature is trying to force our attention to our wasteful and destructive ways by showing us her angry face – in all the natural disasters that are occurring with such frequency and anger. Peace is a pipedream! We must mend our ways.

Conclusion

Oh Thou who Man of baser Earth didst
 make
And who with Eden didst devise the
 Snake:
For all the Sin wherewith the Face of
 Man
Is blacken'd, Man's forgiveness give —
 and take!
  Rubaiyat of Omar Khayyam By Edward
  Fitzgerald

The rate at which problems around the world are occurring, envisages to any who would stop a moment and think – a world in conflagration. And then we will go back, much as Nostradamus had foretold – to sticks and stones. I just can't see how the world and its inhabitants can survive a Third World War with all our very advanced technology and weapons. We can only pray that sense prevails and another period of a cold war world is initiated!

The USA should look after the citizens of its own country and stop interfering in the welfare of other countries. No good ever comes from outside intervention in the political or social or any other situation. The only time interference is viable is if there is genuine ethnic cleansing. But at those times the USA does not intervene. Look at the Rohinga crises or the Palestinian issue.

The more USA intervenes in other country especially militarily the less money is there for the US citizens. Moreover, going to war has many negatives results. For one thing you are never certain when or where death awaits you. It is one thing to fight for your country. That is patriotism and much to be commended. But I would not like for my family to go fight someone else's war and perhaps die. Then there is the huge amount of money needed that is much better used for the citizens' needs. Then there is the psychological toll that war especially on foreign soil takes on the soldiers. And finally there is the toll on the families of the soldiers. No one returning from war with its noise and insecurity and killing is ever the same again.

Another thing which I think is especially applicable to immigrants is this: If there is no interference in another country's internal affairs – political or otherwise, countries can rule themselves well. When we exploit other countries, we upset the balance. Foreign country interference always leads to extreme right wing dictators, which in turn leads to instability and internal unrest. When people are constantly watching their backs, while the dictators line their own pockets and thereby bleed the nation – vice abounds especially drug cartels. This in turn leads to people becoming economic and political immigrants. Border walls are not enough to keep out mass immigration. Deal with the root of the problem – do not interfere in other countries' and immigration problems will lessen dramatically.

The USA creates problems in countries where the USA wants to have control. This is wrong, just as it was when Britain, Spain, France and the Dutch and others did earlier. We are not our brothers' keepers.

The USA and its eternal paranoid fear of Marxism leads to baseless problems from time to time. Meanwhile right wing dictatorships are never questioned or attacked with all the serious consequences for the peoples of those countries. Instead they are favoured. When a country has to be destroyed for whatever unhealthy reason, the leader is demoted to the status of a dictator but when there are real dictators like Duarte, Noreiga, Pinocet - the list is long – nothing happens. They are feted and applauded. It is a sad indictment on us that we do so.

And not only in the USA but also in many other countries too division is exacerbated. Populist leaders make this worse by appealing to our baser natures. We do not rise to our potential but cater to the worst in our natures. Democracy cannot and will not function under such circumstances. The gap between the have and have-nots is getting wider and wider. The rock of democracy is foundering very badly in the waters of egoism and parochial sentiments.

We look to our leaders to set a good example for us. We expect them to be better, to lead where we can follow happily without guilt. Our leaders are expected to be an inspiration to us, to have empathy for us and have the ability to inspire us to be the best we can – not to wake up the baser instincts in us, to envy others, to kill for the sake of destroying, to be cruel.

What we now see in the world and most especially in America – being a world leader is dissension, division, destruction that man-supplies as well as nature in reaction to our abuse of the earth, and death. Social norms have been breached and broken. Death hides behind every corner and in safe places like the school, the playground, the church, the home, the shopping centre. No place is safe anymore! We have to stem this tide of our bad behaviour and show that we really are *the roof and crown of things* (Alexander Pope Essay on Man).

I will end on a note of hope for as long as there is life, there is hope. All this will pass, must pass. We must wake up and not get embroiled in a third world war. Though the prognosis looks very bleak for the world, politically with problems in all corners of the earth; economically as the stronger countries try to strangle the weaker countries and no one goes down without a fight; environmentally with all the natural disasters dogging us at every point for our misuse, our abuse and rape of our earth and worst of all socially as people kill their fellow men for nothing at all. This is the worst of all. We use terms that have become meaningless to convince ourselves to commit murder – be it to a country, to other students, to our neighbours. For these sins we must pay the price. But I believe humankind deep down is basically good and soon I hope, we will all wake us to our sacrilege of our fellow human beings and of our beautiful world!

> *Tho' much is taken, much abides; and tho'*
> *We are not now that strength which in old days*
> *Moved heaven and earth, we are*
> *One equal temper of heroic hearts,*
> *Made weak by time and fate, but strong in will*
> *To strive, to seek, to find, and not to yield.*
>
> **Ulysses** by Lord Alfred Tennyson

Anthem for Doomed Youth
By Wilfred Owen

What passing-bells for these who die as cattle?
Only the monstrous anger of the guns.
Only the stuttering rifles' rapid rattle
Can patter out their hasty orisons.
No mockeries now for them; no prayers nor bells;
Nor any voice of mourning save the choirs,—
The shrill, demented choirs of wailing shells;
And bugles calling for them from sad shires.

What candles may be held to speed them all?
Not in the hands of boys, but in their eyes
Shall shine the holy glimmers of goodbyes.
The pallor of girls' brows shall be their pall;
Their flowers the tenderness of patient minds,
And each slow dusk a drawing-down of blinds.

Appendix A

The Foreign Operations, Export Financing, and Related Programs Appropriations Act, 1991, Public Law 101-513, appropriated funds for the fiscal year ending September 30, 1991. Below is the paragraph relating to Yugoslavia:

Sec. 599A. Six months after the date of enactment of this Act,

(1) none of the funds appropriated or otherwise made available pursuant to this Act shall be obligated or expended to provide any direct assistance to the Federal Republic of Yugoslavia, and

(2) the Secretary of the Treasury shall instruct the United States Executive Director of each international financial institution to use the voice and vote of the United States to oppose any assistance of the respective institutions to the Federal Republic of Yugoslavia: Provided, That this section shall not apply to assistance intended to support democratic parties or movements, emergency or humanitarian assistance, or the furtherance of human rights: Provided further, That this section shall not apply if all six of the individual Republics of the Federal Republic of Yugoslavia have held free and fair multiparty elections and are not engaged in a pattern of systematic gross violations of human rights: Provided further, That notwithstanding the failure of the individual Republics of the Socialist Federal Republic of

Yugoslavia to have held free and fair multiparty elections within six months of the enactment of this Act, this section shall not apply if the Secretary of State certifies that the Socialist Federal Republic of Yugoslavia is making significant strides toward complying with the obligations of the Helsinki Accords and is encouraging any Republic which has not held free and fair multiparty elections to do so.

Appendix B

https://www.britannica.com/event/Monroe-Doctrine
Monroe Doctrine
American history
WRITTEN BY:

* The Editors of Encyclopaedia Britannica

See Article History

Monroe Doctrine, (December 2, 1823), cornerstone of U.S. foreign policy enunciated by Pres. James Monroe in his annual message to Congress. Declaring that the Old World and New World had different systems and must remain distinct spheres, Monroe made four basic points: (1) the United States would not interfere in the internal affairs of or the wars between European powers; (2) the United States recognized and would not interfere with existing colonies and dependencies in the Western Hemisphere; (3) the Western Hemisphere was closed to future colonization; and (4) any attempt by a European power to oppress or control any nation in the Western Hemisphere would be viewed as a hostile act against the United States.

The doctrine was an outgrowth of concern in both Britain and the United States that the continental powers would attempt to restore Spain's former colonies, in Latin America, many of which had become newly independent nations. The United States was also concerned about Russia's territorial ambitions in the northwest coast of North America. As a consequence, George Canning, the British foreign minister, suggested a joint U.S.-British declaration forbidding future colonization in Latin America. Monroe was initially favourable to the idea, and former presidents Thomas Jefferson and James Madison concurred. But Secretary of State John Quincy Adams argued that the United States should issue a statement of American policy exclusively, and his view ultimately prevailed.

The first draft of the message included a reproof of the French for their invasion of Spain, an acknowledgement of Greek independence in the revolt against Turkey, and some further indications of American concern in European affairs. Adams argued for the better part of two days against such expressions, which were finally eliminated from the message.

The ground that I wish to take is that of earnest remonstrance against the interference of the European powers by force in South America, but to disclaim all interference on our part with Europe; to make an American cause, and adhere inflexibly to that.

The Monroe Doctrine, in asserting unilateral U.S. protection over the entire Western Hemisphere, was a foreign policy that could not have been sustained militarily in 1823. Monroe and Adams were well aware of the need for the British fleet to deter potential aggressors in Latin America. Because the United States was not a major power at the time and because the continental powers apparently had no serious intentions of recolonizing Latin America, Monroe's policy statement (it was not known as the "Monroe Doctrine" for nearly 30 years) was largely ignored outside the United States

The United States did not invoke it nor oppose British occupation of the Falkland Islands in 1833 or subsequent British encroachments in Latin America. In 1845 and again in 1848, however, Pres. James K. Polk reiterated Monroe's principles in warning Britain and Spain not to establish footholds in Oregon, California, or Mexico's Yucatán Peninsula. At the conclusion of the American Civil War, the United States massed troops on the Rio Grande in support of a demand that France withdraw its puppet kingdom from Mexico. In 1867—partly because of U.S. pressure—France withdrew.

After 1870 interpretation of the Monroe Doctrine became increasingly broad. As the United States emerged as a world power, the Monroe Doctrine came to define a recognized sphere of influence. Pres. Theodore Roosevelt added the Roosevelt Corollary to the Monroe Doctrine in 1904, which stated that, in cases of flagrant and chronic wrongdoing by a Latin American country, the United States could intervene in that country's internal affairs. Roosevelt's assertion of hemispheric police power was designed to preclude violation of the Monroe Doctrine by European countries seeking redress of grievances against unruly or mismanaged Latin American states.

From the presidency of Theodore Roosevelt to that of Franklin Roosevelt, the United States frequently intervened in Latin America, especially in the Caribbean. Since the 1930s the United States has attempted to formulate its Latin American foreign policy in consultation with the individual nations of the hemisphere and with the Organization of American States. Yet the United States continues to exercise a proprietary role at times of apparent threat to its national security, and the Western Hemisphere remains a predominantly U.S. sphere of influence.

Charles Evan Hughes's article on the Monroe Doctrine appeared in the 14th edition of the *Encyclopædia Britannica* (*see* the Britannica Classic: Monroe Doctrine).

The Editors of Encyclopaedia BritannicaThis article was most recently revised and updated by Jeff Wallenfeldt, Manager, Geography and History.

Bibliography

All web pages used in this book were accessed from April 2019 until end of June 2019.

https://www.washingtonpost.com/politics/trumps-history-of-flippant-misogyny/2015/08/08/891f1bec-3de4-11e5-9c2d-ed991d8 48c48_story.html?utm_term=.8bbcfa6af605
https://www.theguardian.com/us-news/2016/oct/08/trumps-misogyny-problem-how-donald-has-repeatedly-targeted-women
https://antifascistnews.net/2015/07/29/28-racist-sexist-homophobic-and-transphobic-quotes-from-gop-frontrunner-donald-trump/

Political Issues

https://en.wikipedia.org/wiki/Afghanistan
https://borgenproject.org/ten-facts-about-the-afghanistan-war/
https://military.wikia.org/wiki/Death_of_Osama_bin_Laden
DVD *Farenheight 11* by Michael Moore
https://en.wikipedia.org/wiki/United_States_involvement_in_regime_change_in_Latin_America
https.en.wikipedia.org/Wikipedia/IBM_Simon
Cruelty and Silences: War, Tyranny, Uprising & the Arab World Makay.K 1993
https://en.wikipedia.org/wiki/Iraq
https://en.wikipedia.org/wiki/Iraq
https://www.militarytimes.com/news/your-military/2018/08/20/us-to-remain-in-iraq-as-lon
Carnage By Appointment - Maria Seferou 1993 Helsinki Publishers
https://www.britannica.com/place/Iraq/Iraq-under-Saddam-Hussein#ref793758
https://simple.wikipedia.org/wiki/Iraq

https://www.bing.com/search?q=Iraq&qs=n&form=QBRE&sp=-1&pq=iraq&sc=8-4&sk=&cvi

https://www.usip.org/publications/2017/09/current-situation-iraq

www.Xlibris.com.au – *Betrayal* a Political Documentary of our Times by Ashley Smith aka Sophia Z Kovachevich 20012

https://listverse.com/2009/07/11/10-cases-of-american-intervention-in-latin-america/

https://www.bing.com/search?q=us+interference+in+central+america&qs=n&form=QBRE&sp=-1&pq=us+interference+in+c&sc=0-20&sk=&cvid=645A04BF3758406FB1BC6EED0C6B915A

https://www.theguardian.com/commentisfree/cifamerica/2010/jan/29/us-latin-america-haiti-honduras

www.Xlibris.com.au – *Betrayal* a Political Documentary of our Times by Ashley Smith aka Sophia Z Kovachevich 20012

https://progressivevoicesofiowa.com/2017/10/10/us-interventions-have-destabilized-central-america/

https://prezi.com/6iqtxnpxo/problems-in-central-america/

WEB Page Micah Zenko "Clear and Present Safety" https://en.wikipedia.org/wiki/2011_military_intervention_in_Libya

https://foreignpolicy.com/2016/03/22/libya-and-the-myth-of-humanitarian-intervention/

"Libya: UK and French No-Fly Zone Plan Gathers Pace". BBC News. 8 March 2011. *Archived from the original on 20 March 2011. Retrieved 10 March 2011.*

"U.S. Mulling Military Options in Libya". CNN. *2 March 2011. Archived from the original on 7 July 2012. Retrieved 10 March 2011. "Odyssey Dawn: Phase One Of Libya Military Intervention". The Epoch Times. 19 March 2011. Archived from the original on 23 February 2015.*

"Nato Takes Over Libya No-Fly Zone

Martin Chulov (20 October 2012). "Gaddafi's last moments: 'I saw the hand holding the gun and I saw it fire'". theguardian.com. Retrieved 24 September 2016.

https://sputniknews.com/analysis/201904101073965656-us-libya-haftar/

http://www.arabnews.com/node/1480081

The Gaza Strip: The Humanitarian Impact of the Blockade Fact Sheet

"WORKING IN THE GAZA STRIP". UNRWA

"Everything You Need to Know About the Israel-Gaza Conflict". ABC News. 31 July 2014

Tristan Dunning, *Hamas, Jihad and Popular Legitimacy: Reinterpreting Resistance in Palestine,* Routledge

Sara Roy, *Hamas and Civil Society in Gaza: Engaging the Islamist Social Sector,* Princeton University Press, 2013

Arnon, Arie (Autumn 2007). "Israeli Policy towards the Occupied Palestinian Territories: The Economic Dimension, 1967–2007"

Thomas E. Copeland, *Drawing a Line in the Sea: The Gaza Flotilla Incident and the Israeli-Palestinian Conflict,* Lexington Books, 2011

The Palestinians: In Search of a Just Peace, Cheryl Rubenberg – 2003

Sanger, Andrew (2011). M.N. Schmitt, Louise Arimatsu, Tim McCormack (eds.). "The Contemporary Law of Blockade and the Gaza Freedom Flotilla". Yearbook of International Humanitarian Law 2010. Springer Science & Business Media

Gawerc, Michelle (2012). Prefiguring Peace: Israeli-Palestinian Peacebuilding Partnerships. Lexington Books

Jerome Slater, Just War Moral Philosophy and the 2008–09 Israeli Campaign in Gaza, International Security 37(2):44-80 · October 2012

Dennis J. Deeb II, *Israel, Palestine, & the Quest for Middle East Peace,* University Press of America, 2013.

Sara Roy, *Hamas and Civil Society in Gaza*

Between State and Non-State: Politics and Society in Kurdistan-Iraq and Palestine. Springer. ISBN 978-1-137-60181-0.

Samira Shackle (14 October 2013). "Israel tightens its blockade of Gaza for 'security reasons'". Middle East Monitor

Dion Nissenbaum. "Olmert aide supports free Gaza". McClatchy Newspapers. 8 December 2008

"Gaza Strip, overview". Freedom House.

Jonathan Cook, 'How Israel is turning Gaza into a super-max prison,' The National (Abu Dhabi) 27 October 2014

The Palestinians: In Search of a Just Peace, Cheryl Rubenberg – 2003
Dennis J. Deeb II, *Israel, Palestine, & the Quest for Middle East Peace,* University Press of America, 2013.
https://en.wikipedia.org/wiki/Gaza_Strip
https://www.lowyinstitute.org/the-interpreter/how-un-security-council-failed-syria
https://*www.aljazeera.com*/news/2016/05/*syria*-civil-*war*-explained.
https://www.theguardian.com/world/2018/apr/14/syria-conflict-assad-putin-russia-iran-israel#img-1
https://www.bing.com/search?form=MSNSBE&mkt=en-au&PC=MI9P&qs=n&sk=&q=syria
https://www.bbc.com/news/world-middle-east-26116868
https://www.dw.com/en/yemen-conflict-all-but-ignored-by-the-west/a-37157913https://www.bbc.com/news/world-middle-east-42008809
https://www.bbc.com/news/world-middle-east-29319423
https://www.independent.co.uk/news/world/middle-east/yemen-war-civilian-deaths-injuriesAl Jazeera News
https://www.dw.com/en/syria-and-yemen-gaping-wounds-in-the-middle-east/a-36963373
https://www.dw.com/en/yemen-conflict-all-but-ignored-by-the-west/a-37157913
https://www.washingtonpost.com/immigration/hundreds-of-minors-held-at-us-border-facilities-are-there-beyond-legal-time-limits/2019/05/30/381cf6da-8235-11e9-bce7-40b4105f7ca0_story.html?utm_term=.461026d4aed9
https://www.insider.com/immigrant-children-testimonies-border-facilities-conditions-2018-7
https://en.wikipedia.org/wiki/Monroe_Doctrine
https://www.axios.com/inside-border-facility-detention-centers-migrant-children-us-mexico-0c5ea20e-623a-4546-b0d1-10bde69b2901.html
A Century of U.S. Intervention Created the Immigration Crisis by Mark Tseng-Putterman
https:// https://en.wikipedia.org/wiki/List_of_United_States_military_bases

htts.com/inside-border-facility-detention-centers-migrant-children-us-mexico-0c5ea20e-623a-4546-b0d1-10bde69b2901.html

Trump & Politics

hhttps://thinkprogress.org/trump-plays-dumb-about-right-hand-salute-f790c20b6d52/
ttps://www.aljazeera.com/indepth/opinion/cost-xenophobia-trump-america-180803091125432.html
https://www.theatlantic.com/politics/archive/2015/07/donald-tr
https://www.independent.co.uk/voices/donald-trump-us-elections-mexicans-germophobia-a7237971.html
https://www.axios.com/inside-border-facility-detention-centers-migrant-children-us-mexico-0c5ea20e-623a-4546-b0d1-10bde69b2901.html
https://newrepublic.com/article/124295/america-nation-xenophobic-trumps   https://*www.thenation.com*/article/*trumps-xenophobic-vision-of-america-is-*inciting
https://www.theatlantic.com/politics/archive/2017/01/donald-trump-scandals/474726/
https://*www.washingtonpost.com*/blogs/post-partisan/wp/2015/11/23/
Betrayal
A Political Documentary of Our Times – Ashley Smith
Economic Issues
https://www.nato.int/cps/ua/natohq/topics_68144.htm
https://en.wikipedia.org/wiki/World_Trade_Organization
https://www.politico.eu/article/jim-mattis-resignation-donald-
https://www.google.com/search?client=firefox-b-d&ei=LL1jXIbyOJGo9QP9r5SIAw&q=nato+purpose&oq=NATO&gs_l=psy-ab.1.1.0i7l18.0.0..155970...0.0..0.0.0.......0......gws-wiz.7evcZRYJL3s
https://www.trtworld.com/americas/trump-s-top-five-withdrawals-from-international-agreements-18543
https://www.state.gov/t/avc/trty/102360.htm
https://apnews.com/4d7b80a285a04d18b116af413d07a2d1)

https://www.cnbc.com/2018/08/10/why-trump-is-attacking-turkey-with-sanctions-and-tariffs.html

https://www.theguardian.com/world/2018/mar/22/china-us-sanctions-trade-war

https://www.google.com/search?client=firefox-b-d&q=KORUS

https://www.heritage.org/trade/report/analyzing-the-renegotiated-us-korea-free-trade-agreement-korus

https://www.google.com/search?client=firefox-b-d&q=NAFTA

https://en.wikipedia.org/wiki/Group_of_Seven

https://www.internationalrelationsedu.org/what-is-the-g7-its-purpose-and-history-of-influence/

https://www.theatlantic.com/international/archive/2018/06/trump-g7/562493/

https://www.aljazeera.com/news/2018/06/withdraws-human-rights-council-180619173311272

https://www.smh.com.au/world/europe/us-poised-to-announce-exit-from-un-human-rights-council-20180620-p4zmi5.html

https://journal-neo.org/2019/01/19/us-withdrawal-from-nato-would-benefit-americans-most-of-all/

http://www.un.org/en/universal-declaration-human-rights/

https://www.state.gov/r/pa/prs/ps/2017/10/274748.htm

www.Xlibris.com.au – *Betrayal* a Political Documentary of our Times by Ashley Smith aka Sophia Z Kovachevich 20012

www.bbc.com/news/world-u-canada-43902372

https://www.bbc.com/world-u-Canada-43902372

www.Xlibris.com.au – *Betrayal* a Political Documentary of our Times by Ashley Smith aka Sophia Z Kovachevich 20012

Moscow (Sputnik)

https://www.independent.co.uk/news/world/middle-east/iran-tanker-attack-mine-gulf-oman-japan-oil-us-evidence-uk-a8965181.html

Massacre/Shootings websites

https://www.statista.com/statistics/476381/school-shootings-in-the-us-by-victim-count/

https://docs.google.com/spreadsheets/d/1b9o6uDO18sLxBqPwl Gh9bnhW-ev_dABH83M5Vb5L8o/edit#gid=0
https://en.wikipedia.org/wiki/Category:Mass shootings in the United States by year
https://www.gunviolencearchive.org/reports/mass-shooting
https://www.vox.com/world/2019/3/14/18266624/christchurch-mosque-shooting-new-zealand-gunman-what-we-know
https://en.wikipedia.org/wiki/Mass shootings in the United States
https://en.wikipedia.org/wiki/List of massacres in New Zealand
https://www.statista.com/statistics/476381/school-shootings-in-the-us-by-victim-count/
https://en.wikipedia.org/wiki/List of massacres in Australia
https://www.abc.net.au/news/2015-03-09/quakers-hill-nursing-home-fire-inquest-findings-released/6290248
https://www.abc.net.au/news/2016-08-05/rozelle-shop-owner-adeel-khan-sentenced-to-30-years-jail/7692802
https://www.statista.com/statistics/476381/school-shootings-in-the-us-by-victim-count/
https://en.wikipedia.org/wiki/Category:Mass shootings in the United States by year
https://www.presstv.com/Detail/2019/03/24/591817/US-school-shooting-survivors-commit-suicide
https://*docs.google.com*/spreadsheets/d/1b9o6uDO18sLxBqPwl Gh9bnhW
https://www.abc.net.au/news/2014-12-16/sydney-siege-gunman-two-hostages-dead/5969162
https://www.statista.com/statistics/476381/school-shootings-in-the-us-by-victim-count/
https://en.wikipedia.org/wiki/Category:Mass shootings in the United States by year
https://www.presstv.com/Detail/2019/03/24/591817/US-school-shooting-survivors-commit-suicide
https://*docs.google.com*/spreadsheets/d/1b9o6uDO18sLxBqPwl Gh9bnhW

www.ingramcontent.com/pod-product-compliance
Lightning Source LLC
Chambersburg PA
CBHW051438250726
48655CB00001B/127

* 9 7 8 1 7 9 6 0 0 5 6 2 2 *